DATE DUE

APR 1 0 1972			
NOV 27			
OCT 24 1974			
NOV 5 1978			
DEC 1 1 1989			
OCT MAY 4 1993			
MAY 2 1 1993			
GAYLORD			PRINTED IN U.S.A.

HAWTHORNE'S
CONTEMPORANEOUS REPUTATION

A Study of Literary Opinion
in America and England
1828-1864

By

BERTHA FAUST

1968
OCTAGON BOOKS, INC.
New York

Originally published in 1939

Reprinted 1968
by special arrangement with Bertha Faust
OCTAGON BOOKS, INC.
175 FIFTH AVENUE
NEW YORK, N. Y. 10010

LIBRARY OF CONGRESS CATALOG CARD NUMBER: 68-17371

Printed in U.S.A. by
NOBLE OFFSET PRINTERS, INC.
NEW YORK 3, N. Y.

I wish to express my deep appreciation to Dean Paul H. Musser for his aid and counsel in this work, and to acknowledge my debt to Professor Arthur Hobson Quinn, to whose devotion American literature owes so much. I wish also to thank Professor Stanley Williams, of Yale University, at whose suggestion I undertook the critical study of Hawthorne.

FOREWORD

THIS study of Nathaniel Hawthorne's reputation covers the period from 1828 to the end of 1864—that is to say, from the publication of *Fanshawe* to a time sufficiently extended beyond the date of Hawthorne's death to include most of the comments occasioned by that event. It is based chiefly upon notices and articles in the magazines and reviews of the period, in America and Great Britain. Criticism of Hawthorne's work found in contemporaneous books is also included. To this are occasionally added the opinions of Hawthorne's readers and acquaintances as they appear in letters and memoirs, and some newspaper comment where it seems significant. The material is arranged in chronological order except for a few instances where the desire for coherence has suggested a slight deviation; and it is elucidated, where necessary, by biographical and literary references.

The aim of the study is to show Hawthorne as he appeared to the eyes of his contemporaries, to trace the progress of his literary reputation during his lifetime, and also, in a measure, to give a general impression of the state of critical thought in America and England, and to reveal the spirit of the age as it is reflected in a particular facet.

HAWTHORNE'S
CONTEMPORANEOUS REPUTATION

PART I

BEFORE THE SCARLET LETTER

THE first public reference to Nathaniel Hawthorne as an author occurred in 1836, in the *American Monthly Magazine,* although it was then eight years since he began to publish his writings. The more significant part of our study begins with that notice, but we shall first deal briefly with the early years of anonymity. They present some points of interest.

Hawthorne's inclinations toward literature seem to date from an early period in his life and the dream of literary reputation was persistent in his boyhood. There is a letter to his mother, written before he entered college,[1] which throws an interesting light upon his young ambition. He runs through the list of the professions, divinity, law and medicine, remarking on his disinclination to each, and ends by asking: " What do you think of my becoming an author, and relying for support on my pen? " He adds, " Indeed I think the illegibility of my handwriting very author-like. How proud you would feel to see my works praised by the reviewers, as equal to the proudest productions of the scribbling sons of John Bull. But authors are always poor devils, and therefore Satan may take them." He has put last what was first in his mind, and has phrased his suggestion with that affectation of carelessness and that real diffidence which is characteristic of his later sayings about his profession and his writing, but it is obvious from other indications that the thought of a career of authorship was constantly in his mind. The reference to the scribbling sons of John Bull shows that he had imbibed, perhaps from the very air about him, the nationalistic interest in literature which was one of the signs of the times, and had acquired the conviction, very widely and deeply held, that the American nation could in no respect more plainly

---

[1] Dated March 31, 1821. See *Nathaniel Hawthorne and his Wife* (1:106–108).

7

and defiantly reveal her independence of England than by producing a literature surpassing that of the mother country. Hawthorne's boyish aspirations and early versifying might be brushed aside as common enough at that time and in that place,—that is to say, in a society which, though simple, was cultivated and intensely conscious of the importance of the written word; but when one considers that he had no other serious ambitions, either during his school and college days or later, it becomes evident that his purpose, however sluggish in its manifestations, was immovably fixed upon one object. As Lathrop points out, the passage in *Fanshawe* in which the hero is discovered as actuated by the dream of undying fame has a definite autobiographical value; and it may be more representative of Hawthorne's true feelings than his more explicit statements about his work and his choice of a profession, in which he always speaks, as it were, in the character of a dilettante.

The history of Hawthorne's earliest attempts in literature is obscure and need not concern us here. If his sister's recollections are not entirely inaccurate, he practiced writing prose while in college. Be that as it may, Hawthorne returned to his mother's house in Salem in the summer of 1825; and in the autumn of 1828 he published *Fanshawe*.[1]

Fanshawe was published anonymously at Hawthorne's expense (one hundred dollars) by Marsh and Capen at Boston—a modest volume modestly put out, and, as a private venture of its author, quite in accordance with that respectable habit of selling one's own wares which was the foundation of New England's industrial prosperity. One may readily see, however, that as a commercial venture it was not very well advised. Goodrich was later of the opinion that it might have done better in better hands, but the nature of the story was against it. To be sure, novels of somewhat less art and no greater pretensions had been sold, but they had different qualities. For the most part they were either more romantic or more *instructive,* to use the contemporary word. *Fanshawe's* mildly romantic atmosphere could scarcely appeal to that quaint taste which made *Alonzo and Melissa,* with its thrice-distilled absurdities, the most popular (or the most popular but one) of our early novels. On the other hand

---

[1] *Fanshawe. A Tale.* Boston: Marsh and Capen. 1828. 12mo., pp. 141.

Fanshawe lacked the homely touch and the direct persuasion to virtue which gave Miss Sedgwick's *A New England Tale* a certain degree of success, and which recommended a number of works of a similar kind, if without similar merit, to a public still generally suspicious of fiction which did not edify.

In the year in which *Fanshawe* was published Cooper put forth in *Notions of the Americans* [1] some reflections upon the difficulties under which American literature was struggling. The first difficulty, he said, lies in the fact that American publishers find it cheaper and safer to reprint English books for nothing, than to pay their countrymen for their writings and then run the risk of failure with an untried book; and the second obstacle lies in the poverty of materials for the artist. America, he observed, has no annals for the historian, no follies for the satirist, no manners for the dramatist, no obscurification for the writer of romance, no gross and hardy offenses against decorum for the moralist, nor any of the rich artificial auxiliaries of poetry—" no costume for the peasant (there is scarcely a peasant at all), no wig for the judge, no baton for the general, no diadem for the chief magistrate." This dismal catalogue, which sounds strangely like Henry James' more famous lament over the flatness of American civilization, comes oddly from the pen of a writer who had discovered and exhibited to the admiration of mankind a fresh and absorbing field of romance in his own country. It does not apply to Cooper's own work (his modesty in this respect was absolute and he quite unconsciously leaves it out of consideration) but it does apply with some precision to the sort of romance which Hawthorne attempted to write. Romance of the kind written by Scott or by Mrs. Radcliffe or by Gœthe was impossible, unless on the plane of absurdity, in an American setting. *Fanshawe* is not absurd, and therefore it is tame. Hawthorne thus found himself faced, in his first attempt, with both of the obstacles mentioned by Cooper, the practical and the artistic.

Two comments on *Fanshawe* have been discovered, one in the *Ladies' Magazine* and one in the *Critic*. That there are only two is owing partly, no doubt, to the fact that copies for review had not been very widely or systematically distributed and partly to the fact that at the moment there were few American periodicals which made a prac-

---

[1] *Notions of the Americans Picked up by a Traveling Bachelor.* .Philadelphia 1828.   (2:106–107.)

tice of reviewing fiction of the lighter kind, or indeed of any kind. The two periodicals in which notices appeared were both in their first year, and one of them, as it happened, in its last—two differing off-spring of the rising enthusiasm for magazine publication, which has set, in the ensuing years, so many frail ventures upon the uncertain sea of journalism. The *Ladies' Magazine* was edited, and largely written, by Sarah Josepha Hale, then in the beginning of her fabulous editorial career. It was a very personal journal, seriously devoted to its editor's lifelong cause—female education.

The review of *Fanshawe* appeared in the issue of November 1828.[1] Mrs. Hale remarks that she had intended to give a rather long notice of this work and to prove the correctness of her favorable opinion by several extracts. But time and space being lacking, she must there-fore briefly commend the book " to all those who wish to encourage the talents of our native writers." She adds: " But do not depend on obtaining it for perusal from a circulating library, or from a friend. Purchase it, reader. There is but one volume, and trust me it is worth placing in your library." " The time has arrived," she continues, " when our American authors should have something besides empty praise from their countrymen. Not that we wish to see a race of mere book-worm authors fostered among us. Our institutions and character demand activity in business: the useful should be preferred before the ornamental; practical industry before speculative phi-losophy; reality before romance. But the emanations of genius may be appreciated, and a refined taste may be cultivated among us, if our people would be as liberal in encouraging the merits of our own writers, if they would purchase the really excellent productions which depict our own country, scenes and character, as they do the vapid and worn-out descriptions of European manners, fashions and vices." She ends her notice with an additional recommendation to buy the book, and with a quotation from Fanshawe's reflections upon his newly discovered love. The style of the article is characteristic of its writer and destined to become very well known. It has a tone at once familiar and serious, an inimitable air of appealing kindly and severely to the better natures of its feminine audience. In this case the appeal is to the patriotism of the reader and to the patriotic conviction of America's superior moral position; and it was inspired, there can be

---

[1] *Ladies' Magazine* (1:526–527) November 1828.

no doubt, by a sympathy, more professional than sentimental, for the difficulties besetting the path of an aspiring American author. Mrs. Hale had also tried her hand at authorship, with financial results not as rewarding as they should have been.

The *Critic,* a weekly, was, like the *Ladies' Magazine,* a personal organ. It was founded, edited and largely written by William Leggett, who was just beginning his stormy journalistic career; and it was composed ambitiously on the model of the English literary and theatrical weeklies. Very soon after the review of *Fanshawe* appeared the *Critic* was sold out to the popular and unambitious *New York Mirror,* and its editor joined William Cullen Bryant on the *Evening Post.*

Leggett's article begins:[1]

> Who wrote this book? Yet what need is there to know the name of the author, in order to pronounce a decision? Be he whom he may, this is not his first attempt, and we hope it will not be his last. The mind that produced this little interesting volume is capable of making great and rich additions to our native literature; and it will, or we shall be sadly mistaken.

The author, says Leggett, is a scholar, though there is no display of scholarship, a poet though there are few metrical lines, a gentleman though he writes about a country college. His heart is alive to the beauties of nature and the beauties of sentiment. His language is simple, chaste, and appropriate, " describing all the beautiful and varied traits of the landscape in which he has chosen to locate his narrative; describing the heavens in all their different aspects of storm and sunshine, in the gray twilight of morning, the sleepy splendor of noonday, and the gorgeous effulgence of sunset and describing (a more difficult thing to do) the human heart both as it lightly flutters in a young pure happy maiden's bosom, and as it heavily beats beneath the yellow and shrivelled skin of an octogenarian virago; both as it animates the dark recesses of a ruffian's breast, and the young, ardent impetuous bosom of an honorable and thoughtless lad of eighteen." This, says Leggett, requires a poet. He points out, however, that there are some faults in the book. The plot lacks probability; there is too much villainy in some of the characters; and the character of the principal of Harley College is a caricature. As proof of merit Leggett

---

[1] *Critic* (1:53–55) November 22, 1828.

quotes the deathbed scene with the remark that the book is not in a tone as sombre as the quotation might indicate, though poor Fanshawe will sometimes excite the reader's tears in spite of himself. Leggett concludes:

We love to read and love to review a work like this, where we can conscientiously shake hands with the author and bid him, All hail, and be sure on leaving him, that no unkindly feelings have been created to rankle his breast, making both the critic and the criticised unhappy. Besides those already mentioned we have no fault to find with the author of *Fanshawe*, but we shall have, if he does not ere long give us an opportunity of reading one of his productions. Is it not quite possible that Willis wrote the book? We merely *guess*.

This final guess was far wrong, and rather less wrong in its estimate of the work than its estimate of the character of the suggested author. Willis had too just an appreciation of the value of having one's name before the public to publish an anonymous work at this stage of his career. Still the suggestion was distinctly complimentary, for Willis was regarded at this date, in New York at least, as a rising star. The whole article is as kind and complimentary as possible, though a little, as it were, beside the point. Leggett has evidently been pleasing himself with his own fine writing, and the phrases about " the gorgeous effulgence of sunset " and the varieties of " the human heart " are somewhat inappropriate in describing a work which is marked by Hawthorne's characteristic sobriety of tone and modesty of appeal, if by no other element of his later style. The reference to " our native literature " should be noted. It pairs with Mrs. Hale's reference to " our native authors." Both are manifestations of national feeling.

Mrs. Hale and Leggett were interested in the cause of American literature as a cause, and in this they were not, of course, unusual. It may be said that, where no personal or political quarrel was involved, any American book would receive a friendly notice, if it received a notice at all. In Mrs. Hale's case it is quite evident that the native origin of *Fanshawe* was its chief recommendation. In the *Ladies' Magazine* and later in *Godey's* she seldom failed to review the *Token* of the year; and in these reviews she never mentioned any piece of Hawthorne's. She will single out a tale of John Neal or of Mrs. Sigourney for praise, but the numerous tales and sketches of the author whom she had praised at unusual length (most of her literary notes are decidedly jotty, and she seldom quotes, except from works dealing with the education of women or with household economics) are passed over in silence.

Hawthorne was not encouraged by these two notices, though both were as kind as the heart could desire. More solid encouragement was lacking. Mrs. Hale's readers apparently did not follow her advice; and the book had almost no sale. This outcome, though it was, as we have pointed out, highly probable under the circumstances, was deeply humiliating to the author. He seemed to regard it as a judgment on the merit of his novel; and he recalled all the available copies and destroyed them. *Fanshawe* nevertheless did Hawthorne good service. It impressed Goodrich sufficiently to cause him to inquire after the anonymous author, according to his own account.[1] That is to say, it presumably introduced Hawthorne to a publisher, and provided him with the opportunity for marketing his wares which he was apparently too proud or too inexperienced to seek for himself.

Samuel Griswold Goodrich was best known as Peter Parley—that is, as the publisher and nominally the author of a long series of phenomenally successful books of information for children. His publishing interests however embraced a number of fields, and included the *Token,* which soon became the most successful of the American annuals, quite outstripping the numerous competitors in this curious form of periodical publication and absorbing, in 1832, the most respectable of its rivals, the *Atlantic Souvenir.* His relations with Hawthorne became somewhat strained in time (there were a number of irritations) but at this period, as Woodberry points out, he was Hawthorne's most useful friend. He not only sought out Hawthorne of his own accord, but he remained convinced of the merit of his work and continued to publish it in the face of the fact that it was apparently of no especial advantage to his publishing house, and at a time when other publishers would have been hard to find. The editors of the *Atlantic Souvenir,* in any case, showed no interest in Hawthorne's work when he offered it to them. Goodrich later performed the useful service of recommending Hawthorne's writing to the editors of the *New England Magazine,* and thus, as we shall see, gave him a magazine connection.

---

[1] See his *Recollections,* p. 270.

The earlier parts of the extensive correspondence in which Goodrich says he engaged Hawthorne are not available. The first letter we possess is dated January 19, 1830.[1] In it Goodrich praises the manuscripts which Hawthorne had submitted, especially " The Gentle Boy " and " My Uncle Molineaux." He is more doubtful about public appreciation of " Alice Doane." He promises that he will use his influence to induce a publisher to bring out his work, remarks that *Fanshawe* might have been successful if it had been in better hands, and " as practical evidence of my opinion of the uncommon merit of these tales " offers thirty-five dollars for the privilege of inserting " The Gentle Boy " in the *Token.* If he uses " The Gentle Boy," he notes, he will return " Roger Malvin's Burial."

In May of the same year there is a letter from Hawthorne offering two pieces for the *Token,* with the suggestion that they might be published as by the author of *Provincial Tales,* which was the title Hawthorne intended giving the volume to which Goodrich's letter had referred. He adds in explanation: " An unpublished book is not more obscure than many that creep into the world, and your readers will suppose that the ' Provincial Tales ' are among the latter." One of these pieces must have been " Sights from a Steeple," which appeared in the *Token* for 1831 ; the other *may* have been one of three or four anonymous sketches in the *Token* of that year which have been attributed to Hawthorne at various times. Or possibly there may have been more than two of Hawthorne's works in this *Token.* The Old Manse edition includes two of the attributions, " The Haunted Quack " and " The New England Village " ; and if these are accepted, there would be three pieces in all. However that may be, Goodrich in the following year seemed more firmly convinced of the value of Hawthorne's work. A letter of May 31, 1831 gives notice that he is inserting four tales in the *Token* for 1832, and contains the following interesting passage : [2]

As they are anonymous, no objection arises from having so many pages by one author, particularly as they are as good, if not better, than anything else I get. My estimate of the pieces is sufficiently evinced by the use I have made of them, and I cannot doubt that the public will coincide with me.

----

[1] See *Nathaniel Hawthorne and his Wife* (1:131).
[2] See *Nathaniel Hawthorne and his Wife* (1:132).

The four tales referred to (which appeared in due course in the *Token*) were " The Wives of the Dead," " My Kinsman Major Molineaux " (this as by the author of " Sights from a Steeple "), " Roger Malvin's Burial " and " The Gentle Boy."

On the publication of the volume in October Goodrich wrote, " I am gratified to find that all whose opinion I have heard agree with me as to the merit of the various pieces from your pen." These opinions were evidently informal and private; for the tales, so far as we have been able to ascertain, occasioned no public comment whatever. There were, of course, few extended notices of the volume. In this year as in others there was an occasional line in a newspaper—a bit of perfunctory praise for the *Token* as a whole, with, more rarely, a word about the " embellishments " and a partial list of the better-known contributors. In the magazines the *Token* was, for the most part, either ignored or simply listed among new publications. Mrs. Hale gives a few lines to the *Token* of this year, with a favorable mention of Miss Sedgwick. On the more solid side of literary criticism, there is a notice in the *American Monthly Review*,[1] a periodical of serious ambitions, founded by Sydney Willard, who resigned the chair of Hebrew at Harvard to undertake its editorship. The reviewer remarks of the *Token:* " It has some prose with little meaning, and more poetry, with less," but somewhat modifies his general verdict by commenting favorably on a tale called " My Wife's Novel," and by agreeing with Mrs. Hale that Miss Sedgwick's " The Blue Stocking " is an excellent story. " My Wife's Novel " has been attributed to Hawthorne and it is included in the Autograph Edition: but the attribution is doubtful in the extreme; and, even granting its validity, the tale is less characteristic of its supposed author and less meritorious than any one of the four tales which are unquestionably Hawthorne's, and which are quite overlooked by the reviewer. These notices (the *Ladies' Magazine* and the *American Monthly Review*) may be regarded as typical of the comments occasioned by the *Token* both in this year and in the ensuing three years, although there were at least three of Hawthorne's tales in the *Token* for 1833 (" The Seven Vagabonds," " Sir William Pepperel," " The Canterbury Pilgrims ") and three more in the *Token* for 1835 (" The Haunted Mind,"

---

[1] *American Monthly Review* (11:154) February 1852.

" Alice Doane's Appeal," " The Mermaid "). That is to say, until the *Token* for 1836 appeared, no one singled out one of Hawthorne's pieces, by a single word.

This silence and lack of recognition, which applies with slight modification to the whole period of Hawthorne's connection with the *Token* as well as to these early years, requires a little explanation. The tales which appeared in the *Token* are among Hawthorne's best; and the *Token* was, as we have said, the best known and the most respectable, in a literary sense, of the American annuals. Yet it provided Hawthorne with very poor means for the display of his talents. The anonymity of the tales is one reason, undoubtedly, why they were not noticed; another is, that the annuals were rather lightly regarded and not read with studious attention; but a third reason lies in the nature and the contents of the annuals.

It had become the fashion in these publications, beginning with the *Atlantic Souvenir* of 1826, to present the work of American authors; and by the time that Hawthorne appeared as a regular contributor to the *Token,* the leading annuals usually boasted that they contained nothing but native writing. This limitation of authorship somewhat restricted the range of tone and subject matter. We have quoted Goodrich as telling Hawthorne that his tales were as good, or better, than anything else he got. The statement is interesting. The pieces are as good as, or better than, others, but it is implied that they are in the same vein. In spite of the fact that most of the tales were not written for the *Token* (they were intended for a collection to be published in book form) they fall roughly into the types of writing that were in current vogue in the annuals. American colonial history, for instance, was frequently employed, either for itself or as the background for some incident, by the tale writers of the day. Such tales as " Sir William Pepperel," " The Gray Champion," and " The May Pole of Merry Mount " fall, by virtue of their subject, into this very usual category. Furthermore Hawthorne's studies of eccentricities of character, his portraits of persons dominated by a single idea or by a single passion, have parallels in the annuals. Nearly all of John Neal's numerous tales deal with some form of " monomania," although his description usually ends with a dubiously mirthful turn. There are a number of serious treatments of this kind of subject to be discovered. " The First Born " by Richard Penn Smith, in the

Atlantic Souvenir for 1831, is a good example,—a gloomy account of punishment visited on insane pride. Willis also, in his own manner, made a good deal of eccentric character. Thus " Roger Malvin's Burial," " Young Goodman Brown," " Wakefield," " The Minister's Black Veil " and " The Wedding Knell " struck no decisively new note. Their rivals in the field may have been for the most part either artless and amateurish efforts, or insincere and uninspired hack-work, but they had the advantage of being more direct and highly colored. Their lack of sublety and refinement made for a more immediate appeal. In another field, that of the descriptive essay, Hawthorne's work suffered again from the sober delicacy of its treatment. " Sights from a Steeple " and the later essay " Sunday at Home " really represent Hawthorne's most " original " contributions to the *Token*. No other essays ever appeared in it, unless one counts the brief reflections (usually very silly) which sometimes accompanied the plates. But if " Sights from a Steeple " was unusual in its form, it was of all Hawthorne's pieces the least calculated in its style and its subject to attract casual attention.

The unsuitableness of the *Token* as a means for placing Hawthorne's work before the public may be estimated, in fine, by Goodrich's assertion that Willis was its most valuable contributor. Goodrich ascribed Willis' popularity to the fact that his temperament was " all sunshine and summer "; and he asserts that Hawthorne's lack of success was owing to contrary qualities—to his " gloom." This cannot be the whole explanation, for " gloom " has always enjoyed a certain degree of popular favor, and was never in higher favor than in the thirties of the last century, when America, like the rest of the world, was still enchanted by the Byronic spell. The reason lies rather in the fact that there is nothing " taking " in Hawthorne's manner—no obvious appeal to the eye of the reader. Willis is all captivation. His writings are in one respect the antithesis of Hawthorne's: they are written with calculated appeal by one who made it his business to know the tastes of his public. The readers of the *Token* were charmed by his art. The larger reading public was also dazzled, and we find only an occasional conservative, like Cooper, who resisted it upon other grounds than those of professional jealousy. The labored satire upon the New York literati in *Home as Found* is directed against the shallowness and affectation of the group to which Willis belonged, which offended Cooper not so much in his capacity of critic as in his instincts of a gentleman.

The *Token* for 1836 contained three of Hawthorne's tales, " The Wedding Knell," " The May Pole of Merry Mount," and " The Minister's Black Veil "; and Hawthorne's work drew for the first time some attention,—two notices from two oddly different sources.

Goodrich had introduced Hawthorne's writing to Dr. Samuel Howe and John Sargent, the editors of the *New England Magazine,* and incidentally to Park Benjamin, who was then assistant editor and in March 1834 became sole editor and proprietor of the magazine. It was Park Benjamin, apparently, who suggested that the incomplete materials of the *Story-Teller,* a collection which Hawthorne had hoped to print in a volume, be published in his magazine. The story which was intended as an introduction to the volume was printed in the *New England Magazine* of November and December 1834 under the title " Passages from a Relinquished Work," and in 1835 some of Hawthorne's work appeared in every issue of the *New England Magazine* except that of September: some fourteen separate pieces in all, including " The Gray Champion," " Young Goodman Brown," " Wakefield," " The Ambitious Guest," " The Old Maid in the Winding Sheet," " The Vision of the Fountain," and " The Devil in Manuscript." " The Gray Champion " was printed as by the author of " The Gentle Boy "; and thereafter most of the tales were ascribed to the author of " The Gray Champion." A number of the pieces including the " Rill from a Town Pump " were unascribed, and " The Devil in Manuscript " was attributed to Ashley A. Royce. Park Benjamin, then, in noticing Hawthorne's work in the *Token* for 1836, was merely paying a compliment to the most constant contributor which his magazine possessed.

The compliment was a very modest one. The review of the *Token and Atlantic Souvenir* which appeared in the *New England Magazine* for October [1] runs to some length, but it is devoted chiefly to abuse of the editor of the volume, under the transparent title of Mr. Parley Vous. It is in Benjamin's best waspish style, perfectly developed at this period though then not as well known as it was later to become.

---

[1] *New England Magazine* (9:294–298) October 1835.

He accuses Goodrich of buying favorable notices of his publications
by giving away copies; and remarks that although Goodrich has not
ventured to send him a copy of the *Token,* he will criticize the volume
with impartial justice and without regard to the desert of an editor
" whom we look upon as occupying the same rank in literature as a
quack vendor of universal nostrums in medicine." He then proceeds
to ridicule the poetry at length, and to pronounce a modified con-
demnation of the engravings. The prose articles, which were noted
at the beginning as somewhat more tolerable than the poetry, have two
sentences devoted to them. " The author of the ' Gentle Boy ' whom
we regard as the most pleasing writer of fanciful prose, except Irving,
in the country, and ' John Neal ' have displayed their usual freshness
and originality. ' The Young Phrenologist,' by the latter, is very pretty,
but slightly *inuendoish* (to adopt the author's own fashion of coining
words) and ' Anacreon Mooreish.' " This half sentence devoted to
Hawthorne's writing cannot be regarded as over-generous in view of
the fact that the reviewer as editor had received a great deal of good
work from him, at very low rates. However Benjamin, as his ready
acceptance of the work shows and as his later expressions prove, was
an admirer of Hawthorne's. His admiration (never a very active
faculty in his nature) was here swallowed up by his indignation
against Goodrich, which at this moment was raised to a high pitch by
the fact that he was financially interested in an annual which was an
unsuccessful competitor of the *Token.*

The second notice is found in the *Athenaeum* [1] and is from the pen
of Henry Chorley, then in the third year of his long association with
that journal. It begins with a few words on the illustrations of the
Token, giving the artists credit for good intentions. " The letter
press by which they are accompanied calls for no such allowance, being
fully equal to the average standard of the annual prose and verse of
the old country." Miss Sedgwick's and Miss Leslie's tales are noted
as being pleasant. " Connected with these, we have two stories of
darker colour ' The Wedding Knell,' and ' The Minister's Black
Veil,' each of which has singularity enough to recommend it to the
reader." Chorley then gives an extended series of quotations from
" The Maypole of Merry Mount," with a note on the oddity of find-

---

[1] *Athenaeum* (pp. 830–831) November 7, 1835.

ing "our old friends the Cavaliers and Puritans" in a new world setting.

The praise bestowed in this article on Hawthorne's writing is not overwhelming, it will be seen; and yet in the absence of any similar notice in America it is remarkable and worth noting. Chorley was later to felicitate himself, with justice, upon his acumen. The remarkable aspect of the article does not lie in the comment but in the fact that Chorley had singled out all three of Hawthorne's tales. He could not have known that "The May Pole of Merry Mount" was by the same author as "The Wedding Knell" and "The Minister's Black Veil"; and nevertheless he was aware, if only moderately, of the superiority of the three tales. His perspicacity is owing as much to his geographical advantage as to his critical talents. Chorley was not especially remarkable, at any point in his career, for the originality of his views, or for his ability to recognize merit in an unfamiliar form. But in this case he had the advantage of being relatively unfamiliar with the current forms of American literature. We have said, in discussing the annual, that the fact that Hawthorne made use of the material and the forms employed by other American writers tended to obscure his work in the mass of similar writing. The fact that Chorley was less acquainted with these materials made the mass seem less homogeneous. The "singularity" of the tales was more readily apparent to him than to an American reader. There was besides, in England, a decided interest in the American scene. Part of Cooper's great success, aside from other valid considerations, was owing, no doubt, to the fact that he was depicting a world in which strangeness and familiarity were blended, and which, in being both strange and familiar, was fascinating. Chorley evidently was struck by the native quality of Hawthorne's writing and by his individual and picturesque use of local material.

Hawthorne was much gratified by this English appreciation, and properly enough, for it was not inspired by favor, either national or personal. It did not, of course, contribute to his popular reputation, but it probably impressed those whose notice was drawn to it, Park Benjamin and Goodrich for instance. Aside from the fact that the *Athenaeum* had a deserved reputation for great probity in literary matters, the English review was a thing of great estimation in America, both at this period and for a long time afterward. Lowell was not greatly exaggerating when he made his typical minor author say,

"—for you know 'tis
The whole aim of our lives to get one English notice;
By American puffs I would willingly burn all

*   *   *

To get but a kick from a transmarine journal! "

Hawthorne's chief claim to popular success at this time came from the " Rill from a Town Pump." This essay was widely (though of course anonymously) reprinted in newspapers. Its attraction lay in its subject which is, or which seemed to be, an argument against intemperance. As an unusual presentation of an old question it drew a good deal of attention at the moment of its appearance, and its popularity as a piece of temperance literature continued for some time. It was later reprinted as a tract and obtained a large circulation in England as well as in America.

Goodrich was sufficiently encouraged, in any case, to publish eight tales and sketches by Hawthorne in the *Token* for the following year —" Monsieur du Miroir," " Mrs. Bullfrog," " Sunday at Home," " The Man of Adamant," " David Swan," " The Great Carbuncle," " Fancy's Show Box," and " The Prophetic Pictures." The fact that a large portion of the volume was written by one author was concealed by leaving three tales without ascription, and by assigning the others variously to the author of " The Gentle Boy," to the author of " Sights from a Steeple," to the author of " The Wives of the Dead," and to the author of " The Wedding Knell." He paid Hawthorne one hundred and eight dollars for these contributions—that is to say, considerably less than he would have been obliged to pay to a writer of some reputation. He was, as it were, taking advantage of a bargain. These pieces, however, seemed to arouse no more public attention than the previous ones. The only discoverable notice of the *Token* which mentions Hawthorne's work is one by Park Benjamin in the *American Monthly Magazine*.[1]

This review was owing partly to considerations other than pure literary appreciation. During his term as editor of the *New England*

---

[1] *American Monthly Magazine* (n. s. 2:405–406) October 1836.

Magazine Benjamin had, as we have said, received a good deal of writing from Hawthorne, and some of it was not paid for, even at the rate of a dollar a page, which was the standard remuneration for contributions. When at the end of the year Benjamin joined forces with Charles Fenno Hoffman in the *American Monthly Magazine,* he apparently begged from Hawthorne some unpublished manuscripts for his new venture, which were, according to Horatio Bridge, " scornfully bestowed." Benjamin thus owed Hawthorne a debt of gratitude; and he was willing to pay it, for, though irascible, he was not ungenerous. His anger at Goodrich had besides partially subsided. The review states that the *Token* for 1836 is " very creditable to the publisher and, in many respects, creditable to the editor." The embellishments are some good and some bad, but the stories are superior to those of any previous *Token.*

The author of " Sights from a Steeple," of " The Gentle Boy," and of " The Wedding Knell," we believe to be one and the same individual. The assertion may sound very bold, yet we hesitate not to call their author second to no man in the country except Washington Irving. We refer simply to romance writing, and trust that no wise man of Gotham will talk of Dewey, and Channing, and Everett, and Verplanck. Yes, to us the style of NATHANIEL HAWTHORNE is more pleasing, more fascinating than anyone's except their dear Geoffrey Crayon. This mention of the real name of our author may be reprobated by him. His modesty is the best proof of his true excellence. How different does such a man appear to us from one who anxiously writes his name on every public post. We have read a sufficient number of his pieces to make the reputation of a dozen of our Yankee scribblers: and yet, how few have heard the name above written! He does not even cover himself with the same anonymous shield at all times; but liberally gives the praise which, concentrated in one, would be great, to several unknowns. If Mr. Howthorne would but collect his various tales and essays into one volume we can assure him that their success would be brilliant—certainly in England, perhaps in this country. His works would, probably, make twice as many volumes as Mr. Willis's. How extended a notoriety has the latter acquired on productions, whose quantity and quality are both far inferior to those of this voluntarily undistinguished man of genius!

This fling at Willis reenforces a scathing article in the same issue of the magazine on Willis's prose and another in the previous issue on his poetry. Having delivered the irresistible thrust, Benjamin resumes his subject by remarking that the *Token* would be worth its cost for

the three tales " Monsieur du Miroir," " The Man of Adamant,"
and " The Great Carbuncle " " if every other piece were as flat as
the editor's verses." He identifies " David Swan," " Fancy's Show
Box," and " The Prophetic Pictures " as by " the same graphic hand."
" The Great Carbuncle " is eminently good, he says, and, like the rest
of its author's tales, it " conveys an important moral." The editor,
continues Benjamin, is to be congratulated upon having followed the
advice given in the *New England Magazine,* which was, to rest his
claims on the merits of the contributions rather than on the celebrity
of the contributors; and in fact " we can think of only one method
by which he can do better than he has done:—this is, next year to
employ Hawthorne to write the whole volume, and not to look at it
himself till it be for sale by all booksellers in town and country."

The review is important because it contains the first public mention
of Hawthorne's name; though it scarcely brought the name into
prominence. For the rest, it says at length what Park Benjamin's
previous notice had said briefly: that Hawthorne is, after Irving, the
most pleasing writer of fanciful prose in the country. The assertion
was not as modest as it sounds to us: " fanciful prose " was then, one
might say, the staple of American letters, and it had a great number
of practitioners, prominent and obscure. In any case, the notice of
Park Benjamin marks the end of the period of strict anonymity. In
March of the following year the long-projected collection was to be
published, under the name of its author, and though Hawthorne continued to publish anonymously in periodicals, his status as an author
by profession became somewhat more regular.

Of this period Hawthorne's later designation of himself as the ob-
scurest man of letters in America is accurate enough. While it is
probably not true that (as Park Benjamin implies) he might have
acquired a wide reputation by signing his works, yet the carefully
maintained anonymity was indubitably a factor in the lack of public
recognition. Horatio Bridge [1] scolded him on at least two occasions
for not publishing under his own name. Bridge was quite right from
a practical point of view, since a reputation, however small, would
have made Hawthorne's work commercially more valuable. Anonymity was, of course, common enough in this period, when, in spite of

---

[1] See *Nathaniel Hawthorne and his Wife* (1:138 and 141).

the great importance laid upon the profession of literature, professional authorship was still looked upon with a touch of eighteenth-
century distrust. Anonymity was usual in the case of those authors
(often ladies) who wrote presumably for their own amusement. Edward Everett and Longfellow both wrote pieces for the *Token* and for
publications like the *Token* without signing their names; but their
situations were not like that of Hawthorne. They did not propose
to support themselves by such writing, and their literary ambitions lay
in other fields. They could afford to look on an occasional tale for
an annual partly as practice and partly as diversion. Anonymity was
not usual nor advisable in the case of an author who was attempting
to make a livelihood by writing tales. Quite on the contrary: writers
like Willis and Poe and Park Benjamin rightly regarded the compe-
tition for the lean literary rewards that America offered as a tooth-
and-nail struggle which required all their wits as well as all their
talents.

In these seven or eight years the only spontaneous tributes that we
have to record are those of Mrs. Hale and William Leggett on the
theme of *Fanshawe* (though we should possibly include Goodrich in
this category), and of Henry Chorley and, oddly enough, of Margaret
Fuller on the theme of the tales. There is a report that Margaret
Fuller's attention was attracted by a piece in the *Token* for 1832,
and that she made inquiries after the new *authoress*.[1] It is remarkable
on the other hand that all the persons to whom Hawthorne's work
was introduced agreed enthusiastically as to its merits. Goodrich had
no difficulty in persuading the editors of the *New England Magazine*
that Hawthorne's writing was unusually good, and, when in 1836 he
presented his protégé to the *Knickerbocker Magazine,* he found Lewis
Gaylord Clark, then in the third year of his long editorship, in immediate agreement. Clark accepted three items which were published
during the course of 1837—" The Fountain of Youth " (which is
called " Dr. Heidegger's Experiment " in *Twice-Told Tales*), " A
Bell's Biography " and " Edward Fane's Rosebud "; and he wrote
Hawthorne a kind and complimentary letter on the appearance of
the first of them.[2] Others to whom Goodrich appealed were equally

---

[1] See Conway's *Life*, p. 39.
[2] *Nathaniel Hawthorne and his Wife* (1:133). Dated Jan. 4, 1837.

or even more impressed. He records in his *Recollections* [1] that he became " annoyed, almost angry " at the blank silence which greeted Hawthorne's pieces, and wrote " several articles in the papers " directing attention to them (these articles incidentally, if published, are not discoverable) ; and that at last, finding no echo of his views and doubting his own judgment, he asked John Pickering to read some of them. John Pickering, who was one of Boston's most distinguished citizens and one of the most learned men of his day, though not a scholar by profession, said that the tales displayed " a wonderful beauty of style, with a kind of double vision, a sort of second sight, which revealed, beyond the outward forms of life and being, a sort of spirit world," though he thought they were " too mystical to be popular." Goodrich must also have showed the work to Charles Folsom, the librarian of the Boston Athenaeum, for there is a graceful letter extant [2] in which Hawthorne thanks Folsom for " some very kind words respecting some of my productions, which were communicated to me by S. C. Goodrich."

Hawthorne's writing apparently received words of praise from all those whose attention was drawn to it. It did not, for reasons we have discussed, draw attention to itself.

Goodrich in the meanwhile had been bestirring himself somewhat in Hawthorne's practical interests. In 1836 he gave him some hackwork to do in the form of an editorship of *The American Magazine of Useful and Entertaining Knowledge* (the fact that his salary was largely unpaid infused a note of coldness into their relations) and later employed him in compiling *Peter Parley's Universal History on the Basis of Geography.* (This volume, edited jointly by Hawthorne and his sister, was one of the most successful of the Peter Parley series and had an enormous sale.) He also undertook to find a publisher for a collection of tales. The publisher was the American Stationers' Company, a recently formed joint-stock company in which Goodrich had a large interest. The company had been established with the purpose of furthering the publication of native American works and, partly from the misguided enthusiasm of this purpose, soon fell into bankruptcy. In Hawthorne's case, however, more practical considerations than regard for national glory prevailed. Goodrich

---

[1] Pp. 270–271.

[2] See Randall Stewart's edition of the *American Note Books* (p. 337).

says in his *Recollections* that it was an agent of the company who refused to proceed without a guarantee; but the decision was undoubtedly his own. In this he was quite justified. Hawthorne's writing,
as we have seen, had aroused no public notice. There was nothing
in its reception to warrant the hope of a commercial success. And
even disregarding Hawthorne's own failure to awaken interest, collections of tales by American authors were not common. Aside from
Irving and Paulding (and Paulding chiefly in virtue of having a
collected edition of his works) there were very few. Poe's first collection, *Tales of the Grotesque and Arabesque,* appeared in 1840.
Willis, for all his expanding reputation, published only travel and
poetry in volume form. John Neal, an indefatigable writer for the
periodicals, never collected his tales. Miss Sedgwick had ventured to
put forth a volume, *Tales and Sketches,* in 1835: but her most popular
co-worker in the female department of tale writing, Lydia Maria
Child, did not publish a collection until 1846. When the best known
and most demanded writers of tales hesitated to put their work into
permanent form, it must have seemed unlikely that the collected tales
of an unknown writer would sell.

Horatio Bridge, without the knowledge of his friend, supplied the
demanded guarantee, which was two hundred and fifty dollars or
somewhat more than half of the cost of the edition; and an edition of
one thousand copies was accordingly published, appearing on the sixth
of March, 1837.[1] The title *Twice-Told Tales* is characteristic of
Hawthorne's diffidence, but he did consent to publish the volume
under his own name. It contained only eighteen pieces, out of the
thirty-six which Hawthorne had published up to this time, even if one
leaves out of consideration those which have been ascribed to him.
Nevertheless the collection, though small, was thoroughly representative, and gave an accurate impression of Hawthorne's manner in its
then modest range. It was a fair and favorable presentation.

The volume, as the production of a publishing company which was
promising great things, received a scattering of newspaper notices.
We are told that several newspapers supposed the author's name to be
a pseudonym. This was natural enough. One example of this error

---

[1] *Twice-Told Tales* by Nathaniel Hawthorne. Boston: American Stationers'
Company. John B. Russel. 1837. 12mo., pp. 334.

(if it is an error) is found in a notice in the *Boston Courier* for March 9, 1837.

" Twice Told Tales " is the title of a beautiful duodecimo just published by the American Stationers' Company. It is the production of " Nathaniel Hawthorne " whether a true or fictitious name, we know not—probably the latter.

The only newspaper notice of any length appeared in the *Salem Gazette* for March 14th. It was probably written by the editor, who was indebted to Hawthorne for a number of early contributions, all presumably unpaid, and who was about to increase his debt by reprinting, from time to time, pieces from the volume in question or from Hawthorne's magazine publications. The friendly relation was continued during his residence in Salem, Hawthorne even taking the trouble of writing the Courier's New York Addresses for 1838 and 1839. The tribute, then, is one of friendship, and is full of compliments. It says that the salient merits of Hawthorne's writing are his brilliant imagination, his engaging style, his notable humour, and his fine touches of feeling and fancy. He is earnestly requested to continue with his work.

Friendship gained Hawthorne another tribute in a more significant place. He had sent a copy of *Twice-Told Tales* to Longfellow with a modest note, evidently in the hope that his college acquaintance would in some manner exercise his influence in its favor. The hope was superabundantly fulfilled. Longfellow's article appeared in the July issue of the *North American Review*.[1]

The article is well known, and as characteristic of Longfellow in its style as in its kindness. " When a new star rises in the heavens," he says, " people gaze after it for a season with the naked eye, and with such telescopes as they may find. In the stream of thought which flows so peacefully deep and clear, through the pages of the book, we see the bright reflection of a spiritual star. . . ." This star is newly risen, he continues, and soon the observations of numerous star-gazers will inform the world of its magnitude and its place in the heaven of poetry, " whether it be in paw of the Great Bear, or on the forehead of Pegasus, or on the strings of the Lyre, or the wing of the Eagle." Longfellow himself would say of *Twice-Told Tales*, " Live ever, sweet, sweet book." It comes from the hand of a man of

---

[1] *North American Review* (45:59–73) July 1837.

genius, he says, and everything about it has the freshness of May. It
has been gathered fresh from the secret places of a peaceful and gentle
heart. The book, though in prose, was nevertheless written by a
poet. The author is one who looks upon all things in the spirit of
love, " for to him external form is but the representation of internal
being, all things having a life, an end and aim." To his eye all things
are beautiful and holy " from the hierarchy of the silent saint-like
stars, that rule the night, down to the little flowers which are ' stars
in the firmament of the earth.' " Longfellow here quotes a stanza
from one of his own poems:

> " The infinite form of life are bound in one
>   By love's eternal band.
> The glow-worm and the fire-sea of the sun
>   Came from one father's hand."

All things being poetic to the poetic mind, he continues, all poetry is
not in the past with the days of bards, troubadours and minnesingers.
" If poetry be an element of the human mind, and consequently in accordance with nature and truth, it would be strange indeed if, as the
human mind advances, poetry should recede." The past is picturesque
because we see its picturesque and not its commonplace aspects.
Everyday life is full of poetry.

These general remarks, says Longfellow, are intended to give a true
understanding of Hawthorne's character as a writer, for the reader
must look upon life and nature as Hawthorne does in order to judge
the truth and beauty of his sketches. The tales excite a feeling of
personal interest in the author. One of their most prominent characteristics, he continues, is that they are national in character. The
author has wisely chosen his themes among the traditions of New
England, which are excellent materials for fiction. It seems as natural to make tales out of old, tumble-down traditions, as canes and
snuff-boxes out of old steeples, or trees planted by great men. Another of Hawthorne's characteristics, says Longfellow, is the exceeding
beauty of his style. " It is as clear as running waters are. Indeed,
he uses words as mere stepping-stones, upon which, with a free and
youthful bound, his spirit crosses and recrosses the bright and rushing
stream of thought." In this Longfellow remarks that Hawthorne's
style contrasts favorably with that of " some writers of the present

day " who have introduced " a kind of Gothic architecture " into their writing.

Longfellow ends his article by giving a number of quotations from the volume, with enthusiastic words of praise for each. He quotes from " The Vision of the Fountain," from " Sunday at Home," and from the " Rill from a Town Pump," however mentioning that " The Great Carbuncle," which he does not quote, is his especial favorite. These quotations are sufficient, he says, to show the beautiful and simple style of the book, its vein of pleasant philosophy, and the quiet humor, " which is to the face of a book what a smile is to the face of a man."

We may be sure that this article, though written in friendship, was a perfectly sincere expression of opinion, which may be regarded not only as personal, but as representing an opinion which was shared by a number of others. The elaborate and allusive style is characteristic of Longfellow; the sentiments are characteristic of an attitude of mind frequently found among cultivated persons at that time. One might call it sentimental appreciation if the current misuse of the word sentimental did not give the term an unfavorable connotation which the subject does not deserve. The principles of this kind of criticism (if it may be said to have principles) may be more readily absorbed by the impressionistic process from Longfellow's article than categorically specified. In general there was a tendency to prefer sweetness to light, to exalt mood at the expense of thought, to accept (often) purity of intention and personal charm for a clarified artistic result. It acknowledges the great classical sources of inspiration— Shakespeare and Milton and Dante—while emphasizing their softer rather than their brighter aspects, and preferring an intimate knowledge to a scholarly general view. Lowell is perhaps the best representative of the school, which had a number of eminent members both in England and in America; we shall have occasion to speak of him presently. However the practice was necessarily very personal and differs from exponent to exponent, descending on one side of the scale, of course, to bathos. Longfellow in any case remained in the opinions expressed here during his whole life, and continued, as his journals show, to prefer the gentler effusions of Hawthorne's talent, and to choose, as he chooses here, the essays and the simpler moralized tales as his favorites.   Many of Hawthorne's readers agreed with him, as we shall see.

Longfellow's notice was the only one of any importance directly inspired by the publication of the volume.   There are, in fact, very few magazine notices of any kind.   *The Family Magazine,* late in the year, has a few lines,[1] typical in their insignificance, in which the *Twice-Told Tales* are called, " eighteen as pretty little tales as ever were told "; the reviewer adds that no book published in the last year is more worthy of a place in the reader's affections.   Lewis Gaylord Clark, commenting on the *Token* for 1838 in the *Knickerbocker* [2] takes occasion to remark that Hawthorne's writings are " *well* known in every sense."   He points out the excellence of all of Hawthorne's tales in the *Token,* though coupling " Night Sketches Beneath an Umbrella " with a very tame sketch of Martha Washington by Mrs. Sigourney, and devoting most of his space to praise of Pierpont's " The Wonders of the Deep," a florid piece of highly artificial rhetoric.

In the following year Charles Fenno Hoffman was inspired to review his contributor's work.   The article appeared in March,[3] and follows the general outline of Longfellow's remarks, in a style as elevated.   " A rose bathed and baptised in dew—a star in the first gentle emergence above the horizon—are types of the soul of Nathaniel Hawthorne; every vein of which (if we may so speak) is filled and instinct with beauty."   The tales are the offspring of a calm, meditative fancy, he says, intwined at times with a flickering ray of humor. While giving enthusiastic praise to the delicacy and spirituality of Hawthorne's writing, Hoffman goes on to complain of the fact that American literature has largely been composed, so far, of delicacy and spirituality.   He wishes that men endowed with vigorous and sturdy faculties would cast off the fetters of politics and business and give their capacities to nobler tasks.   " We can point to many Apollos, but Jove has not as yet assumed his thunder, nor hung his blazing shield in the sky."   America needs a great literary genius.   " Yet men like Hawthorne are not without their use; nay, they are the writers to smooth and prepare the path for nobler (but not better) visitants,

---

[1] *Family Magazine* (5:280) November 1837.
[2] *Knickerbocker* (10:447–449) November 1837.
[3] *American Monthly Magazine* (n. s. 5: 281–283) March 1838.

by softening and ameliorating the public spirit." Hawthorne's tales, he continues, may easily be misconstrued when they fall into the wrong hands, or are read in an unsympathetic mood; but their restricted character is one source of their charm. " The perusal of *Twice-Told Tales* has excited in us many feelings ' too deep for tears.' We have been led by it to contemplate the author in the twilight of a dim regret, and to picture him to ourselves as a stricken deer in the forests of life." In one kind of writing, Hawthorne reminds Hoffman of Lamb; in another of Irving, partaking " not a little of his picturesque mode of viewing a topic "; in a third kind of writing Hawthorne, in Hoffman's estimation, has no model or predecessor, and the pieces which fall into this type are the " gems and jewels of the work." Hawthorne's manner is individual, he says, and his pathos is redolent of this soil, and native to New England. " The author of *Twice-Told Tales* is an honor to New England and the country." Hoffman ends by hoping for an enlarged second edition of the tales.

The two reviews form an interesting contrast. Hoffman subscribes to Longfellow's praise and partially repeats and amplifies it, though, as a matter of fact, in subscribing to it he distorts it. He mistakes the quality of Hawthorne's writing, which was neither as unworldly, as emotional, nor as sentimental as he describes it. He speaks of *Twice-Told Tales* as if it were merely a superior product of the school of roses and tears—which, after all, it is not—and nevertheless lauds it to the skies. This is quite in order: the sentimental cult had then a literary status, as well as a popular vogue. Even Poe, with all his professionalism and his acerbity, did not question the validity of its claim, and where the claim was reenforced by chivalric considerations, as in the case of women writers, he sometimes sounds like a votary. Hoffman thus gives credit to Hawthorne where he thinks credit is due; but, perhaps with the natural impatience of a man of action, he sighs for better things.

This sigh, with various modulations, echoes and re-echoes through the journals of the period. America needs a literary genius of the first class, says Hoffman. He does not specify the form which the productions of this genius shall take; he merely wishes for something of the Olympian order—something Shakespearean, Miltonic, Homeric —it matters not so that it be grand. This too is quite in order: it was the primary hope and dream of literary America, though, whether from superior complacency or from superior culture, somewhat less operative in the New England group. There are no qualifications in Longfellow's panegyric, and, generally speaking, none in the commendations of any resident of Concord, Cambridge, Boston, or Salem; but Park Benjamin and Hoffman, who represent the professional journalism of the day, both praise Hawthorne's writing while regretfully consigning him to the category of minor writers.

A sprinkling of notices and two reviews, the one by a personal and the other by a professional friend, cannot be regarded as great public attention. However, such as it was, it was effective. The recommendation on the *North American Review,* which for the most part was interested only in serious works or in works of serious importance, had weight; and it met the eyes of those who were disposed by nature or by training to interest themselves in Hawthorne. Poe, who saw everything in the periodical field, saw both notices, and mentally put a black mark after Hawthorne's name for being puffed in the *North American Review,* a journal whose attitude of superiority he detested, and whose contributors he looked on with mingled envy and contempt.

The volume was a success, though hardly a commercial success. It sold at first very moderately and then, no doubt because of Longfellow's review, in greater numbers, and the small edition was almost exhausted within a year. The circle of readers was however sufficiently narrow. J. B. Russel, the printer of the volume, wrote to Hawthorne soon after its publication: " It may be gratifying to you to know that, in addition to the favorable opinions expressed by the newspapers, your book is spoken of in the highest terms by discriminating gentlemen here and at Cambridge." [1] The phrase is illuminating. There were a sufficient number of discriminating gentlemen (and ladies) in Boston and Cambridge to buy out, in the course of time, a small edition. There was, apparently, not a sufficient number of the sufficiently discriminating to purchase another edition of work of the same quality and temper. The second edition was not as readily disposed of.

In spite of the fact that *Twice-Told Tales* thus quietly became the property of the elect, it brought Hawthorne some practical notice. It attracted the attention of John O'Sullivan, who was beginning,

---

[1] See *Nathaniel Hawthorne and his Wife* (1:150–151).

with unbounded hopes, to edit the *Democratic Review,* and who meant his journal to be at once a political force and a literary treasure-house. He invited Hawthorne to contribute, and the first of these contributions, " The Toll-Gatherer's Day," was published in October 1837. The *Democratic Review* became henceforward the chief recipient of Hawthorne's writing, although he continued to publish a few pieces in the *Knickerbocker Magazine* and in the *American Monthly Magazine,* and contributed five pieces to the *Token* for 1838,—" Peter Goldthwaite's Treasure " and " The Shaker Bridal " as by the author of *Twice-Told Tales,* and " Night Sketches Beneath an Umbrella," " Endicott and the Red Cross," and " Sylph Etheredge " anonymously. The pieces which appeared in magazines were now often ascribed to the author of *Twice-Told Tales,* though the larger number were anonymous and two appeared under the perverse pseudonym of Ashley Allen Royce.

We bright briefly list Hawthorne's publications in this period. In the *Knickerbocker Magazine* " A Bell's Biography " appeared in 1837 as by the author of *Twice-Told Tales,* and " Edward Fane's Rosebud " in September. In the *American Monthly Magazine* we find " Fragments from the Journal of a Solitary Man " (anonymous) in July 1837, and a sketch of the life of Thomas Green Fessenden in January 1838 (also anonymous) and " The Three-Fold Destiny " in March, this last as by Ashley Allen Royce. In the *Democratic Review* there appeared " The Toll-Gatherer's Day " in October 1837 anonymously, " Footprints on the Seashore " in January 1838 as by the author of *Twice-Told Tales,* " Snow Flakes " in February anonymously, " Howe's Masquerade " in May as by the author of *Twice-Told Tales,* " Edward Randolph's Portrait " in July anonymously, " Chippings with a Chisel " and a biography of his college friend Jonathan Cilley in September, the one as by the author of *Twice-Told Tales* and the other anonymously, and " Lady Eleanor's Mantle " in December. " Old Esther Dudley," the concluding tale of the " Province House " series, which was published in January 1839, bears Hawthorne's name, being the first publication in any periodical which is directly ascribed to the author. His next contribution to the *Democratic Review,* " John Inglefield's Thanksgiving " in March 1840, is ascribed to the Rev. A. A. Royce. " The Lily's Quest " appeared anonymously in the *Southern Rose* for the nineteenth of January 1839, and the *Boston Miscellany of Literature and Fashion* published "A Virtuoso's Collection" anonymously in May 1842.

On these individually published tales there is, naturally, little traceable comment. O'Sullivan dropped a word here and there in the *Democratic Review* about his contributor. In the editor's preface to the life of Jonathan Cilley he points out that the sketch comes "from a pen whose lighter and more fanciful creations have often charmed the readers of the Democratic Review." [1] In the unsigned "Reminiscences of a Walker round Boston," which was probably written by O'Sullivan, we find a line: "When the Tales of the Province House are narrated by the pen of Hawthorne, who would be ought else than a listener or a reader?" [2]

We do have a remark on "Footprints on the Seashore." Emerson records in his journal that Elizabeth Peabody brought it to him to read. "I complained there was no inside to it. Alcott and he together would make a man." [3] This is Emerson's first comment on Hawthorne and one very characteristic of its maker. His taste in literature was individual, and, as is well known, of an oddly eclectic sort. One may sum it up perhaps by saying that he did not care for art in belles-lettres, but for wit and wisdom. He did not care for the "lighter and more fanciful creations," to use O'Sullivan's phrase, and the airy nothingness of the piece, which was no doubt its chief recommendation in the eyes of its enthusiastic introducer, offended him, the art of its construction being a thing quite indifferent to his spirit. He loved thought, which he blandly appreciated both in its crude and its differentiated state; and, like his beloved nature, he positively abhorred a vacuum—an intellectual vacuum, that is. But his universal wisdom often touched the world of art if it did not embrace it, and upon that subject, as upon most others, he dropped some of the finest observations that have ever been made. It is remarkable, and very characteristic of Emerson, that, thinking little of the art of composition in general and of Hawthorne's practice in particular, he nevertheless made, on a later occasion, what is probably the only piece of contemporary criticism, aside from Poe's, which is purely artistic. [4]

---

[1] *Democratic Review* (3:68) September 1838.
[2] Ibid. (3:80).
[3] See Emerson's *Journals* (4:476).
[4] See pp. 59–60 of this study.

On " The Gentle Boy " we have one or two remarks. Hawthorne had this tale published separately at his own expense, with a drawing by Sophia Peabody, as a tribute to his betrothed.[1] In the *New York Review* (a serious and excellent, if short-lived, review sponsored by a number of Episcopalian clergymen) there was a brief notice in April 1839 [2] which remarked that nothing need be said " of this exquisite story, so generally and deservedly admired " but that it accompanies " an etching after the manner of Retzsch by Miss Sophia A. Peabody which for grace and beauty well merits the approbation it has received from our greatest painter." The drawing had been praised by Washington Allston, and the fact that the reviewer was aware of this marks him as one of the cognoscenti—that is, as one of the small band of—shall we say?—literary acquaintances, who alone could say, speaking for themselves, that the tale was " generally admired." One copy of the small edition wandered as far as London and fell into the hands of a reviewer for the *Literary Gazette* [3] who was not one of the elect. He says simply: " We confess we cannot tell what to make of this sentimental rhapsody. There is a pretty outline illustration."

In the meanwhile a belated review of *Twice-Told Tales* appeared in the *Christian Examiner,*[4] the chief Unitarian journal, once considered radical and now, in its third decade, almost ancient and entirely respectable. The writer was the Rev. Andrew Preston Peabody, who was later to become editor of the *North American Review* and one of the best known of Harvard professors—a writer, even at this date, of astonishing activity. He begins by saying that the mental and moral influence of the most faultless novels and tales of the day is questionable. The fault lies in the kind of composition—a kind which substitutes an unreal world for the world of fact. True poetry, from which higher fiction differs only in form, he continues, takes the world of fact and infuses it with a spiritual glow. " This is the character of the tales before us. For this we prize and admire them. They are poetry from the deepest fountains of inspiration. Their interest consists in the development, not of events, but of

[1] The Gentle Boy. A Thrice Told Tale. By Nathaniel Hawthorne. With an Original Illustration. Boston 1839.
[2] *New York Review* (4: 493) April 1839.
[3] *Literary Gazette and Journal of Belles-Lettres* (p. 303) June 22, 1839.
[4] *Christian Examiner* (25:182–190) November 1838.

sentiment. Many of them have neither plot nor catastrophe, indeed, are not tales in the common sense of the word: but are simply flower-garlands of poetic feeling wreathed around some every day scene or object." He thanks Hawthorne for revealing the hidden harmonies of common things and he is grateful for creations " so full of moral purity and beauty." He is charmed by the " naïveté " of the tales and by the transparency of their style, and feels that he has always been acquainted with the author. The best pieces in the volume, in his opinion, are those which are merely a transcript of the author's own musings. He especially admires " Sunday at Home," " Sights from a Steeple " and " Rill from a Town Pump," but " Little Annie's Ramble " is his favorite of the whole volume. The chief fault of the tales, he says, is that some of them are " too vague and dreamy." The collection in fact is but " a gathering of early wind-falls—the earnest of future rich, ripe, mellow harvests." A mind so rich, a heart so pure, and imagination so teeming with gorgeous fancies awakens the fondest hopes and shows the brightest promise. The tales, he concludes, are full of beautiful phrases and gems of thought, and they have the highest moral tone; they convey touching lessons and beautiful morals, not with set purpose, but from the fulness of the author's heart.

Peabody, we see, echoes Longfellow's sentiments on the poetic nature of Hawthorne's writings, while laying more emphasis, as was natural in his clerical position, on their moral character. He was led to an especial approval of the volume in question partly by the con-temporary deep-rooted distrust of works of fiction in general. When he speaks of the unreal world with which most fiction deals he is not using the term in any philosophical or critical sense. He means sim-ply the world of high life, or, alternatively, the world of romantic adventure, whose representation was generally supposed to unseat the imagination of young readers and make them discontented with their lot. He approves of the fact that Hawthorne's tales entertain the imagination while keeping it at home. The provincial touch appeals to him in quite another sense than it appealed to Longfellow and to Hoffman, who were both sufficiently cosmopolitan in their point of view to recognize the peculiarly New England color of the tales as a valid artistic element. It will be noticed that Peabody prefers pre-cisely the kind of sketch—" Sunday at Home," " Little Annie's

Ramble " and so on—which Emerson complained had " no inside ";
and this preference for moralized fancy was shared by many of Hawthorne's admirers, by the sentimental as well as by the devout. It
coincided with the taste of a day which admired, for instance, John
Pierpont's prose " poems," and thought them profound as well as
spiritual; and the preference has continued (until recently at least)
among those who are interested at once in the moral and the artistic
education of the young,—among the compilers of school readers in
any case.

During this time Hawthorne's friends busied themselves to obtain
him a political post. They seemed to think that his government owed
him a livelihood for his notable and badly paid contributions to literature; but this point of view was apparently not shared by the political
powers. George Bancroft in recommending Hawthorne to the Secre-
tary of the Treasury, described him merely as " the biographer of
Cilley ";[1] and he thus obtained his position of weigher and gauger
in the Boston Custom House, as indeed he obtained his later political
appointments, by party regularity and personal friendship. While
employed at the Custom House, where he spent a little more than two
years, he turned to the production of children's books as means of
supplementing his income. The result was the Grandfather's Chair
series, which was published in three parts by Elizabeth Peabody, who
had set up a kind of transcendental bookshop and homeopathic drug-
store in Boston. The series consisted of *Grandfather's Chair, A
History for Youth, Famous Old People, Being the Second Epoch of
Grandfather's Chair,* and *Liberty Tree, with the Last Words of
Grandfather's Chair,* all published in 1841. The volumes were successful, and were republished in the following year by Tappan and
Dennet. They attracted little critical attention, nor were they intended to attract attention, though Duyckinck in the second issue of his
hopeful journal *Arcturus* gave the first of the series a kindly word.[2]
" The best test of a sentimental author," he remarks, " is the production of a good book for children. If he can write so as to engage
the hearts of both young and old, he must have a portion of the poet's
youthful soul, which grows no older though the furrows on the brow

---

[1] See Jepson, George Edward. Hawthorne in the Boston Custom House.
Bookman (19:573) August 1904.
[2] *Arcturus* (1:125–126) January 1841.

deepen or the world without presses with its cares." He says that those who remember " Little Annie's Ramble " will need no introduction to *Grandfather's Chair*.

Evert Augustus Duyckinck, who had not yet met Hawthorne, was introduced to Hawthorne's writing possibly by O'Sullivan or possibly by his own eager interest in the newer developments in American literature. Lowell was to satirize him, not without some justice, as the general advocate of all unrecognized and unrecognizable geniuses. He was however justified in some of his kindnesses, and notably in his early advocacy of Hawthorne. The works of this undeservedly obscure author, he realized, formed a suitable subject for treatment in his journal, which was intended to be a fresher, livelier, and more influential counterpart of the *North American Review;* and he hastened to prepare an article, which appeared in May 1841.[1]

" In his own peculiar walk of fiction and sentiment," Duyckinck writes, " there is perhaps no author who could supply to us the few natural beautiful sketches of Nathaniel Hawthorne. Of the American writers destined to live he is the most original, the one least indebted to foreign models or literary precedents of any kind, and as the reward of his genius he is the least known to the public." It might be thought, Duyckinck continues, that in a country tenacious of national character and not blessed with many distinguished men of letters, originality and genius would be recognized at once. But it is not so: reputation is dependent upon other qualities than worth. Hawthorne, he says, has no doubt many admirers in New England, and many owe him thanks for passages " of refined sentiment and graceful thought " reprinted anonymously in newspapers, but to the general public he is quite unknown. However, Hawthorne's friends need not regret his lack of popularity, for popularity is not essential to his success. " He has written, not because others admire, but because he himself feels." Hawthorne's writings can bear delay of favor, for they spring from the depths of a true heart. " They are part of the genuine recorded experience of humanity and must live." Though written in the form of tales and sketches, Duyckinck continues, they are poems of a high order and the poetical temperament of their author colors every topic with the hues of fancy and sensi-

---

[1] *Arcturus* (1:330–337) May 1841. Nathaniel Hawthorne.

bility. Hawthorne's genius is peculiar, like that of Charles Lamb. His work is strictly original and, like that of all truly original writers, the solution of a new problem—" the exhibition of the human heart and intellect under a new array of circumstances." Amid " the repulsive anti-poetical tendencies of the present day " his poetical soul speaks in fanciful reveries in tones of gloom and sorrow. The sadness which is the constant attendant of his pen, says Duyckinck, is however the sadness of youth " with naught of the despair of age, or the cold hardness of practical life." There is much of Hamlet in Hawthorne's character—that is to say, a tendency to reflect upon life without energy to enter into it. " His literary life is a fascinated dream, an abstraction." Here Duyckinck quotes from " The Journal of a Solitary Man," to elucidate his point.

" The distinctive mark of Hawthorne's writings," he continues, " is a fanciful pathos delighting in sepulchral images." This taste Hawthorne has in common with several masters of English literature —with Webster " who was originally a sexton," with Jeremy Taylor, and Sir Thomas Browne. " The Wedding Knell " and " The Minister's Black Veil " exhibit " an ingenious refinement of terror, wrought with none of the ordinary machinery of gloom "; they represent " a metaphysical exposition of the dark places of the human soul." Duyckinck quotes the descriptions of Nurse Ingersoll and the White Old Maid, remarking that nevertheless Hawthorne is not an especially gloomy writer: " his melancholy is fanciful, capricious —his spirit of love for all things, his delight in childhood, his reverence for woman, his sympathy with nature, are constant." For if he shows the physician's touch in probing the depths of human sorrow, he has also a fund of cheerfulness and sympathy. Duyckinck concludes by reflecting: " What winning accents he might use from the pulpit—what lay sermons, full of hope and tranquillity and beauty, he may yet give the world in his writings." There is a footnote added to the article in which Duyckinck says he would be pleased to find Hawthorne more popular than he has represented, but that he has mentioned the name to many, some of them book makers as well as book readers, who heard it for the first time.

This essay of Duyckinck's has some excellent points, and it is the best analysis of Hawthorne's art up to this time—sounder, because more pedestrian, than Longfellow's rhapsody. It subscribes to Longfellow's tribute to the poetical aspect of the writing, while bringing out more lucidly its individual qualities. Duyckinck notes the extremely personal nature of the writing and its dependence on the temperament of the writer, which he describes with a great deal of perception, although the terms sound quaint in modern ears. He defines Hawthorne's originality in a satisfactory manner, and he picks out the pieces which are most characteristic, and which have the most valid claim upon critical attention. His criticism belongs to the same school of thought as Longfellow's and it employs, with perhaps inferior grace, the same sentimental terms; but it is stiffened by the solid and amiable common sense which was his distinguishing characteristic in life as well as in letters, and is enlightened by genuine understanding. His use of Hawthorne's own words to explain Hawthorne's character, in the quotation from " The Journal of a Solitary Man," is excellent practice, and has been followed by all serious later critics, who have generally agreed that Hawthorne's singularly open and thoughtful, if singularly unimpassioned, self-judgments cannot be improved. Duyckinck's opinions have thus a permanent value, in that they require, after this lapse of time, no essential revision.

The limited success of *Twice-Told Tales* encouraged Hawthorne to publish a second edition and a second series. It was brought out by James Monroe and Company of Boston in 1842, in two volumes.[1] The first volume contained the same tales as the first edition with " The Toll-Gatherer's Day " added. The second volume contained: " Howe's Masquerade," " Edward Randolph's Portrait," " Lady Eleanor's Mantle," " Old Esther Dudley," " The Haunted Mind," " The Village Uncle," " The Ambitious Guest," " The Sister Years," " Snowflakes," " The Seven Vagabonds," " The White Old Maid," " Peter Goldthwaite's Treasure," " Chippings with a Chisel," " The Shaker Bridal," " Night Sketches," " Endicott and the Red Cross," " The Lily's Quest," " Footprints on the Seashore," " Edward Fane's Rosebud," and " The Threefold Destiny."

Duyckinck, making an occasion of the publication of " The Old Maid in the Winding Sheet " in *Arcturus,* gave Hawthorne a recommendation in advance of his new book by inserting " A Preamble to

---

[1] *Twice-Told Tales.* By Nathaniel Hawthorne. Boston: James Monroe and Company. 1842. 2 vols. 12mo., pp. 331, 356.

Nathaniel Hawthorne "[1] in the section of the magazine which he devoted to editorial comment and called " The Loiterer." He refers to his previous article, summing up his former opinion of Hawthorne as being " one of the most remarkable and original of American authors, his originality growing out of intense self-consciousness and peculiarities of character, as well as the local circumstances by which he was surrounded "; and then reprints Longfellow's article (completely except for its quotations) on the ground that it is more eloquent praise than he himself could achieve.

The first review of the second edition of *Twice-Told Tales* appeared in February in the *Boston Miscellany of Literature and Fashion*,[2] a journal undertaken by a circle of the elect in Boston, and, like some others of a similar kind, very short-lived for all that its editors attempted the light and popular touch. The reviewer, who is probably the editor, Nathan Hale, Jr., speaks consciously for the small cultivated circle of Hawthorne's admirers. The remarks on the tales are those which had now, apparently, become almost standardized. Hale speaks of Hawthorne's preference for " unveiling the movements of the inner man," of his characters which are at once mysterious and real, of his " unearthly light," of his skill in " these dangerous imaginative paths," of his pensive mood and of his delicate humor.

His writings, half tale and half essay, are unique in their form and language. The most engaging simplicity,—in which art wholly conceals the art,—the truest purity of thought and feeling, a warm and kind moral sense, and a polished ease of sentiment and expression, are their constant characteristics.

A notice of the volumes appeared in March in the *Knickerbocker*.[3] Clark says of them that, as many of the tales had appeared in his magazine and excited great admiration, its readers will require no further commendation. He remarks that Hawthorne is an acute and faithful limner of nature, that his mind is like " the plates of a Daguerreotype " and that his writing is very much like Lamb's.

April brought four interesting articles upon the subject of *Twice-Told Tales*. Longfellow faithfully renewed his praise in the *North*

---

[1] *Arcturus* (3:152–155, 394) January 1842.
[2] *Boston Miscellany* (1:92) February 1842.
[3] *Knickerbocker* (19:282) March 1842.

American Review.[1] Lovers of delicate humor, natural feeling, exquisite observation, unerring taste and grace of style, he says, will welcome this enlarged edition, which sustains the high quality of the first. Though Hawthorne has not produced any elaborate work of fiction, his writings are destined to enjoy a permanent and increasing reputation, for they possess that creative originality, "which is the essential life-blood of genius." Hawthorne, he says, gives no copies of English works. " He has caught nothing of the intensity of the French, or the extravagance of the German school of writers of fiction." His writings have the racy flavor of the soil. One of his most remarkable powers (here Longfellow returns to the principal thought in his first article) is his faculty for distilling poetry from everyday life. One of his most characteristic traits is his blending of the natural and the supernatural—never passing the limits of probability though hovering near the dividing line. No other writer resembles him in this. His genius, says Longfellow, is characterized by a large proportion of feminine elements—depth and tenderness of feeling, purity and a certain airy grace. These elements are especially visible in " that exquisite story, which we are tempted to pronounce, as on the whole the best thing he ever wrote "—namely, " The Gentle Boy "; and they are very evident in " Little Annie's Ramble." His female characters are all sketched with great delicacy and loveliness. Hawthorne's range, Longfellow continues, is not very extensive, and his mind is not very versatile. His writing is smooth and quiet; his humor is allied with sighs as well as smiles. Hawthorne is entitled to great praise, Longfellow observes, as a writer of the language merely, for his diction is fresh and vigorous, careful and correct. His thoughts shine through his expression " as through the purest plate glass." Longfellow concludes by saying that Hawthorne's works are now so justly appreciated by all discerning minds that there is no need to commend them again. They are not suitable for " a tumultuous and vulgar popularity " but their tranquil beauty, their truth and healthiness of feeling endear them to the thoughtful few.

The second article is a short review which appeared in the *Boston Quarterly Review* [2] just before that journal lost its curious identity by merging with the *Democratic Review*. It was written by the edi-

---

[1] *North American Review* (54:496–499) April 1842.
[2] *Boston Quarterly Review* (5:251–252) April 1842.

tor, Orestes Augustus Brownson, who was one of the most interesting products of New England's intellectual ferment, a sort of New World Newman who, beginning his career as a Universalist minister, became first an associate of Robert Dale Owen and a founder of the Workingman's Party, and then by gradual change of opinion, an opponent to popular sovereignty and a Catholic. Although throughout his various stages of thought the consistent advocate of unpopular causes, he had nevertheless a fairly extensive circle of readers in New England, and he was able, for a number of years, to publish a journal which was written almost entirely by himself and which was admittedly the mere expression of his personal views. The notice of *Twice-Told Tales,* which is in Brownson's usual lucid and positive style, begins by saying that the tales do not need criticism because their author in his own department is one of those very few men, born to give law to criticism, not to receive the law from it; nor do they need introduction, because no lover of American literature can be presumed to be ignorant of them. " We notice them simply, to tell the author that these tales, excellent as they are, are not precisely what he owes to his country." Hawthorne, he continues, is a genuine artist: he has a creative mind, more creative than that of any American author except possibly Irving; he has an abundance of wit, humor and pathos, an eye " for all that is wild, beautiful, or picturesque in nature," a sympathy with all forms of life, a warm love of humanity, a vigorous intellect and a healthy spirit. " He may be, if he tries, with several improvements, to the literature of his country, all that Boz is to that of England." In fact, Brownson says, he possesses a higher order of intellect than Dickens, as is proved by " The Gentle Boy," which, though a mere sketch, is superior in conception to the character of Little Nell, " confessedly the most beautiful of Dickens' creations." He concludes by enrolling himself among those who regard Hawthorne as fitted to stand at the head of American literature, and by adjuring him to attempt a higher and bolder strain.

The third article is by Duyckinck,[1] who had made Hawthorne's cause his own. He hopes for a third series composed of the tales now appearing in his magazine. " And thus collected, we know nothing to which to compare them, except, perhaps, the German tales of Tieck, as translated by Carlyle." Hawthorne is however truly original—

---

[1] *Arcturus* (3:394) April 1842.

" the master of a perfectly individual style, his own, somewhat confined in its range, but distinguished by select attributes." These
" select attributes " are purity, pathos and sensibility, which, if they
lose something by being always in one vein, are very affecting. " It
would seem to us at times, in the sad and fanciful passages (for Hawthorne writes these), that Mr. Dickens must have seen them, so great
is the resemblance, in such parts, of the two authors. The Little Nell
of the latter is greatly and deservedly admired, but we hazard nothing
in saying, that in the finer portions of sentiment, Hawthorne is fully
equal to the author of the Old Curiosity Shop."

The fourth of the April notices was written by Edgar Allan Poe for
Graham's Magazine.[1] " We have always," he begins, " regarded
the Tale (using the word in its popular acceptation) as affording the
best prose opportunity for the display of the highest talent. It has
peculiar advantages which the novel does not admit. It is, of course,
a far finer field than the essay. It even has points of superiority over
the poem." An accident has deprived him, Poe continues, of his customary space for review (this accident was apparently the appearance
of Longfellow's *Ballads and Other Poems,* to which he had devoted
a long and unfavorable notice) and he must postpone until next
month detailed consideration of *Twice-Told Tales.* He observes
however that America, with the exception of Irving's *Tales of a
Traveller,* has no tales of high merit. " We have had a super-
abundance of the Rose-Matilda effusions—gilt-edged paper all
couleur de rose; a full allowance of cut-and-thrust blue blazing melo-
drama, a nauseating surfeit of low miniature copying of low life, much
in the manner, and with about half the merit, of the Dutch herrings
and decayed cheeses of Van Tuyssel—of all this—*eheu jam satis!*"
Poe objects to the title " Twice-Told Tales " as a double misnomer,
in that the tales are now thrice told and in that most of the so-called
tales are not tales but essays. Nevertheless no American prose composition can compare with some of the articles, and none of them
would do dishonor to the best of the British essayists. " ' The Rill
from the Town Pump ' which, through the *ad capatandum* nature of
its title, has attracted more of public notice than any one other of
Mr. Hawthorne's compositions is perhaps the least meritorious."
Among the best, in Poe's opinion, are " The Hollow of the Three

---

[1] *Graham's Magazine* (20:254) April 1842. Virginia Edition (11:102–104).

Hills," "The Minister's Black Veil," "Wakefield," "Mr. Higginbottom's Catastrophe," "Fancy's Show Box," "Dr. Heidegger's Experiment," "David Swan," "The Wedding Knell," and "The White Old Maid." Hawthorne's style is very pure and his tone effective and in accordance with his themes, though there is insufficient diversity in those themes. "His *originality* both of incident and of reflection is very remarkable, and this trait would assure him at least *our* warmest regard and commendation." The essays, Poe says, are not so novel, but on the whole Hawthorne is one of the few men of indisputable genius that America has produced.

The May issue of *Graham's* [1] contains an expansion and elaboration of this short notice. Poe begins by repeating his captious objection to the title, and then proceeds to discuss the essays. "They are each and all beautiful, without being characterized by the polish and adaptation so visible in the tales proper." Their chief characteristic is *repose,* which exists simultaneously with high originality of thought. "At every turn we are met with novel combinations; and yet these combinations never surpass the limits of the quiet. We are soothed as we read; and withal is a calm astonishment that ideas so apparently obvious have never occurred or been presented to us before." Hawthorne differs in this, says Poe, from Lamb, Hunt and Hazlitt, who have less true novelty of thought than is generally supposed, and whose originality has "an uneasy and meretricious quaintness." Hawthorne's writing has more originality than Irving's and compared with the *Spectator* has "a vast superiority at all points." In short the essays are the product of a "truly imaginative intellect, restrained and in some measure repressed, by fastidiousness of taste, by constitutional melancholy, and by indolence."

Turning to the tales Poe repeats his assertion that the tale affords the best prose medium for the exercise of high talents, and then goes on to explain his well-known theory of "totality" in art—a theory elsewhere dealt with in his critical writings, though nowhere more succinctly set down. The best employment for the highest genius, he says, is a poem which may be perused in no more than an hour; the next best employment is a short prose tale. In these forms the reader's attention may be held without interruption or weariness. Poe then proceeds to explain the proper construction of a tale. The artist first

---

[1] *Graham's Magazine* (20:298–300) May 1842. Virginia Edition (11:104–113).

conceives a certain unique or single effect and then invents incidents to produce it. Every word should count toward his aim; and the result should be neither too brief nor too long. Poe repeats his statement that with the exception of Irving and Hawthorne, there are few American tales of real merit, adding that, while some of John Neal's tales have vigor and originality, they are " diffuse, extravagant and indicative of an imperfect sentiment of Art." Hawthorne's tales belong to the highest region of art. " We had supposed, with good reason for so supposing, that he had been thrust into his present position by one of the impudent cliques which beset our literature, and whose pretentions it is our full purpose to expose at the earliest opportunity; but we have been most agreeably mistaken." Hawthorne's distinctive trait is originality—a trait which in fiction is worth all the rest. Originality as frequently displays itself in novelty of tone as in novelty of matter; and Hawthorne is original in all points. Here Poe runs through the list of tales which he had previously given, with a word of praise for each, though he objects to " The White Old Maid " and " The Minister's Black Veil " as too mystical. He picks out " The Hollow of the Three Hills," not as displaying higher talent than the others, but as giving an example of the author's peculiar ability in treating a commonplace subject. " Not only is all done that should be done, but (what is perhaps an end with more difficulty attained) there is nothing done which should not be. Every word *tells,* and there is not a word which does *not* tell." Poe remarks of " Howe's Masquerade " that it contains a plagiarism, and follows this remark by citing a passage from it and a passage from " William Wilson " in which only his own fantastic interest in the subject of plagiarism could see an imitation. He ends by saying that he has scarcely a word of objection to the tales, unless that there is a too prevalent tone of mysticism and melancholy, and an insufficient variety of subject. " The style is purity itself. Force abounds. High imagination gleams from every page. Mr. Hawthorne is a man of truest genius."

The four articles, interesting in themselves, are interesting in their differences.

Longfellow's notice is more particularized and more definite than his first essay on Hawthorne; but it repeats the same opinions in a somewhat lower key. Where he once hailed the appearance of a new star in the literary heavens he is now content to remark that Hawthorne's work, although of the highest merit, is not destined for wide popularity. Longfellow reaffirms his preference for the softer and more sentimental pieces, especially for " The Gentle Boy." He makes three perspicuous observations not clearly set forth in his previous article: upon Hawthorne's tendency to exploit the territory between the real and the unreal; upon the feminine elements in his temperament (references to " feminine " qualities in art were common at that period and in that school of criticism, where the term had a more definite and perhaps a more complimentary meaning than it has now) ; and upon the singular purity and precision of his style.

Brownson says in sum that Hawthorne possesses talent of the highest order but that his accomplishments have not done justice to his endowments. He echoes Hoffman's nationalistic sentiments in remarking that America has need of a different order of writing; but he adds, partly in exhortation and partly in compliment, that with application Hawthorne might be able to fill in America the place that Dickens fills in England. Duyckinck, after summarizing in brief his earlier admirable comments, and suggesting a parallel with the tales of Tieck, also refers to Dickens and to Little Nell, but in compliment and not in exhortation. The two references to Dickens are interesting; they remind us that Dickens was then at the height of his great influence, and they show how the intense admiration excited by his novels distorted the judgment of even so sensible a critic as Duyckinck. For the qualities that set the whole world weeping over the sorrows of Little Nell were precisely the qualities that Hawthorne, with all his talent, did not possess—forthright sensibility, open and flowing emotion.

We come last to Poe and observe at once that his criticism is of an entirely different kind from that displayed by the three other critics. Their comment is appreciative; his is technical. One might say that, in one sense, his is classical while theirs is romantic. If the terms are vague, the distinction is not. Longfellow, Duyckinck and Brownson are romantic critics in that they follow that impressionistic style of criticism which was engendered by the romantic movement, and which gradually but completely replaced that old criticism of rules and measure which (whether or not it was followed in practice) had formerly dominated literary thought. Poe's criticism is not classical in the sense that it follows Aristotle, Horace or Boileau. It is highly original and strictly *sui generis*. But it is classical in the sense that it is dominated by set conceptions, in that it depends upon strict definitions, and in that it attempts to set a formal standard of excellence. It bristles with rules. Poe is at least as positive as Aristotle, and he is decidedly more didactic than Pope. In this he is like no other American or English critic of the period. His comment upon the art of tale writing as set forth in this essay is, of course, well known and frequently quoted. It is one of the most brilliant manifestations of his critical talent.

These four articles mark the end of the notices directly inspired by the publication of *Twice-Told Tales,* though there is a sprinkling of comment through the next few years. James Russell Lowell took advantage of his brief editorship of the *Pioneer* to drop a favorable word upon the *Historical Tales for Youth,*[1] expressing his gratitude in that " a man of acknowledged genius " had undertaken to write such a book for children in the face of the common belief " that no elderly male or female (of good character) could be too stupid to write a book for children." There is a patronizing article by George James, the novelist, upon " American Works of Fiction " in the *Foreign and Colonial Quarterly Review* for October 1843[2] which ends surprisingly with an enthusiastic note upon *Twice-Told Tales.* Hawthorne's work, says the writer, has truth, fancy, pathos and originality; the commonest things are made suggestive by his treatment and " the oldest truths appear clad in a garment of grace and pleasure." Hawthorne, James continues, has a " vein of temperate and poetical elegance, the like of which is possessed by none of our writers of prose—Mrs. Southey perhaps excepted." He concludes by saying that Hawthorne reminds him of Tieck, in spite of the vast difference in the materials used by the two artists.

Poe mentions Hawthorne twice, once in " Marginalia " in the *Democratic Review*[3] and once in " The Literati of New York City " in *Godey's.*[4] The note in " Marginalia " merely repeats briefly and in the pleasantest manner the opinions expressed upon *Twice-Told Tales,* though it ends somewhat more emphatically with the words:—

[1] *Pioneer* (1:41–42) January 1843.
[2] *Foreign and Colonial Quarterly Review* (2:458–488) October 1843.
[3] *Democratic Review* (5:585–586) December 1844. Virginia Edition (15:3–4).
[4] *Godey's Lady's Book* (32:194–195) May 1846. Virginia Edition (15:3–4).

" and although I think him the truest genius, upon the whole, which our literature possesses, I cannot help regarding him as the most desperate mannerist of his day." Hawthorne is introduced in the preface to the *Literati* as an example of a man of genius who, because he does not subscribe to the disgusting quackery and puffery of the age, " is scarcely recognized by the press or by the public, and when noticed at all, is noticed merely to be damned by faint praise." Hawthorne's field is limited, Poe continues, " yet in this walk he evinces extraordinary genius, having no rival in America or elsewhere—and this opinion I have never heard gainsaid by any one literary person in the country. That this opinion, however, is a spoken and not a written one, is referable to the facts, first, that Mr. Hawthorne *is* a poor man, and second, that he *is not* an ubiquitous quack."

O'Sullivan, who was eager to obtain an office for Hawthorne, asked Duyckinck to " write him up " in the *Democratic Review;* and Duyckinck responded with his usual readiness. The article [1] begins with a reminder that poets are almost always badly paid and continues with a dissertation upon the duty of republics toward their men of letters. Duyckinck then proceeds to speak of Hawthorne's literary qualifications, not however in as glowing terms as one might expect. Hawthorne, he says, has passed that period of his life in which it is necessary to present a systematic examination of his writings. His position is established; " he is admitted to be a genuine author, simple, natural, and perfect in his peculiar department of writing," though Duyckinck does not exalt him with the " gods of the upper air "—with Shakespeare, Milton, Dante and so on. Duyckinck notices the combination of masculine and feminine qualities in Hawthorne's genius. The perfection and unity of his treatment, he says, are masculine; the light play of fancy, the sentiment, are feminine. However, " there is a deeper vein which no woman could ever reach, an intimacy with the sterner powers of life which we should wish no woman to attain." Beneath his smooth style there is more than the fancy of an agreeable essayist. " There is a deep moral sentiment and an original exhibition of the elements of character which mark the author to some extent as a creator." Duyckinck speaks at some length of the fascination exerted " by the occasional gloom and pale glimpses as it were of fiends stealing upon the page." Hawthorne is moreover

---

[1] *Democratic Review* (16:376–384) April 1845. Nathaniel Hawthorne.

in some respects " as keen a moralist as tempest-stricken Lear." Here
Duyckinck quotes a large part of " Young Goodman Brown "; and
then, lest the reader be appalled by this " night-piece," he quotes
" Little Annie's Ramble " with the note: " Such writings as these
are sure to find their way to the heart." He refers with pleasure to
the passage on Hawthorne in the *Foreign and Colonial Quarterly
Review;* hopes to have more volumes of *Twice-Told Tales* and ends
with the summarizing sentence: " A truly pure, gentle and acceptable
man of Genius is *Nathaniel Hawthorne!* "

In the two years following the publication of the second edition of
Twice-Told Tales Hawthorne contributed many tales and sketches
to periodicals. In 1843 there were two of his sketches, " The Old
Apple Dealer " and " The Antique Ring," in *Sargent's New Monthly
Magazine;* there were six pieces in the *Democratic Review*—" The
New Adam and Eve," " Egotism or the Bosom Serpent," " The
Procession of Life," " The Celestial Railroad," " Buds and Bird
Voices " and " Fire Worship "; two (" The Birth Mark " and " The
Hall of Fantasy ") in James Russell Lowell's superior but short-lived
Pioneer; and one (" Little Daffydowndilly ") in the *Boys' and Girls'
Magazine.* " The Celestial Railroad " met a fate like that of the
" Rill from a Town Pump," and may dispute the title of the earlier
piece to the honor of being Hawthorne's most popular work among
his contemporaries, though neither brought him any personal credit.
It was reprinted twice in pamphlet form soon after it appeared (of
course anonymously and without recompense to the author) and continued for a long time to be a popular item among the offerings of the
American Sunday School Union. It also enjoyed a newspaper circulation. Like the " Rill from a Town Pump " it had the air of being
an improving work, and it was eagerly seized upon by those religious
persons (a large body) who felt mistrust and resentment toward the
current " liberal " trend in doctrine. Even Emerson, who was not an
admirer of the liberals if he was their prophet, somewhat relaxed his
attitude toward Hawthorne's writings to comment favorably upon
" The Celestial Railroad." It has, he wrote to Thoreau, " a serene
strength which we cannot afford not to praise, in this low life." [1]

Aside from " The Celestial Railroad " the magazine pieces attracted

---

[1] Thoreau, H. D. *Familiar Letters* (F. B. Sanborn, ed.) Boston 1894 (p.
120).

little attention, though their merit drew some favorable opinions even in quarters remote from the influence of the Concord group. Poe followed up his article in *Graham's* by inviting Hawthorne to contribute to a periodical which he was then planning. William Cullen Bryant, according to his biographer, remarked upon them: [1]

"Have you read (he once said to me) the tales of one Hawthorne (almost an unknown writer then) in the 'Democratic Review'? They are wonderful and the best English written on either side of the Atlantic."

In 1844 there were six pieces in the *Democratic Review*—"The Christmas Banquet," "The Intelligence Office," "The Artist of the Beautiful," "A Select Party," "A Book of Autographs," and "Rappaccini's Daughter." *Graham's* published "Earth's Holocaust," *Godey's* "Drowne's Wooden Image," and the *Child's Friend* "A Good Man's Miracle."

In the following two years the volume of his writing fell off and we have only "P's Correspondence" in the *Democratic Review,* though Hawthorne employed some time in editing Bridge's *Journal of an African Cruiser,* and the "Papers of an Old Dartmoor Prisoner." Hawthorne found it impossible to keep up a continuous stream of production for the magazines. However, early in 1846 (and this in spite of the fact that the second edition of *Twice-Told Tales* had sold slowly and brought him no profit) Hawthorne gathered up eleven of his published pieces, added a long introductory essay "The Old Manse" and called the volume, which appeared as part of Wiley and Putnam's Library of American Books, *Mosses from an Old Manse.*[2]

Mosses from an Old Manse was received by the *Athenaeum*[3] with as much pleasure as any "puffing" American editor could show. Chorley began:

We have had occasion lately to dwell with pleasure on the faëry tales of Andersen; and Mr. Hawthorne's stories for "children of larger growth" have been (as our readers know) equally welcome to us—and on similar grounds. Their unworldliness is charming. While nothing is so revolting as acted sim-

---

[1] Godwin, Parke. *A Biography of William Cullen Bryant.* New York 1883 (1:371).
[2] *Mosses from an Old Manse.* By Nathaniel Hawthorne. In two parts. New York: Wiley and Putnam 1846. 12mo. Two parts bound as one.
[3] *Athenaeum* (pp. 807–808) August 8, 1846.

plicity—unless it be acted philanthropy—there is no teacher to whom we love better to listen than one whose sympathies and convictions have been cherished and matured apart from the crowd; and who, not therefore ceasing to love his species, looks upon them—yet is not one of them. Prejudice must, of course, under such circumstances, be allowed for;—the shadow of thought, if not austerity, from amid which the recluse looks out, causing him to see the sunshine by which others are surrounded through its own dark medium. We must be pre-pared, too, for a far-sightedness which is apt to grow morbid—inasmuch as it substitutes speculation for action. Nevertheless, it is to teaching from " Old Manses " where Poets " dwell apart," that we owe some of our best pleasures.

In addition to the perfection of Hawthorne's tone, says Chorley, there is much to content the reader in the manner in which the legends are presented.

Few prose writers possess so rich a treasury in the chambers of their imagina-tion; while our author's riches never make him extravagant. He gives us what suffices for our thorough enchantment and fullest credence—but nothing more.

Chorley points to " Rappaccini's Daughter " as an example of Haw-thorne's art, remarking that an inferior writer would have spoiled it by heaping horror on horror.

Mr. Hawthorne only leads us by imperceptible degrees into the fearful garden, full of its sumptuous blossoms—then insinuates the dark sympathy between the nature of the lady and her sisters, the death flowers—then gradually fascinates us, even as she fascinated her lover, to feel a love and sorrow for the sorceress greater than our terror, and to attend the catastrophe with those mingled feelings which no spell less powerful than Truth's can command. Thus it is with most of Mr. Hawthorne's stories.

Chorley compares Hawthorne to Tieck and to Töpffner, and to another author " far dearer to all Englishmen,"—namely John Bunyan.

In short, we like this writer and his stories well; and we are not afraid that any among the " fit audience," whom the more delicate and thoughtful creators prefer to assemble, will be disappointed if, attracted by our panegyric, they take up the book.

He objects to nothing about the *Mosses* except " the pedantry of their designation " and the author's announced intention to write no more stories. He quotes from the introduction with great appreciation; and remarks that while all the tales are perfect of their kind, " The Celestial Railroad " and " Earth's Holocaust " are in the grandest style of allegory.

The next article of any consequence appeared in the *American Whig Review* in September [1] under the name of Charles Winterfield; it was written, in other words, by Charles Wilkins Webber, former member of the Texas Rangers and future promoter of fabulous expeditions, who was then reposing from his fatigues in the position of associate editor of the *Whig Review*. Webber begins with several pages of massive irony directed against the nationalism of the Jackson school and especially against the tendency to regard exaggeration and extravagance as a laudable trait of national character. He even sees a tendency to allow the style of the frontier and the utterances of the rude Democrats of the back woods (half-horse and half-alligator) to set a national tone. He further protests against the current demand for originality on the part of American authors; dwells upon the advantages of conservatism in national policy, and, as an afterthought, upon its advantages in literature. This brings him to his principal subject.

It happens that we have not only found conservatism, but a good many other things we have asked for, in our national literature, expressed through the pages of Nathaniel Hawthorne. . . . We don't mean to say that Nathaniel Hawthorne is necessarily a " *non-pareil,*" and therefore above or beyond anybody or anything else in all the land! We distinctly say that there are many of our " Native " writers who, in their particular departments of thought and style, surpass him—or rather any particular effort of his—in their chosen and practised line— but we do say, quite distinctly, that taking the plain level of results aimed at and ends accomplished, our author covers the broadest and highest field yet occupied by the Imaginative Literature of the country, and deserves to be set forth, in very many particulars, as " the glass of fashion and the mould of form " to those who come after, at least!

Webber goes on to say that Hawthorne's manly self-reliance, his quiet unobtrusive dignity, is a lesson to some American writers whom he does not name. He comments upon the benevolence of Hawthorne's satire and upon the restfulness of his style and thought. Hawthorne

---

[1] *American Review, a Whig Journal* (4:296–313) September 1846.

has, in sum, the breadth, depth, repose and dignified reliance " which should characterize a truly national literature." Americans must depend upon their own resources; for imitation subjects us to contempt.

Ours must be an honestly American—if it be not too much to say—an Aboriginal Literature! As distinct from all others as the plucked crown and scalp-lock of the red Indian—as vast, as rude, as wildly magnificent as our Mississippi, our mountains or our Niagara—as still as our star-mirroring lakes at the North—as resistless in its roused strength as the tameless waves which tumble in "the vexed Bermoothes" at the South! Without these idiosyncrasies—unless we are high, free, calm, chivalric and stern—who would recognize us in the outward world?

Descending from these heights, Webber remarks that Hawthorne has no affinities with cant and enthusiasm (he quotes the passage from "The Old Manse" which speaks of Emerson and his disciples to prove it) and that, in fact, Hawthorne is a Whig, if only he knew it, and not a Loco-Foco. Webber goes on to particularize Hawthorne's literary traits. One of the finest, he says, is " a sort .of magical subtlety of vision " which compels the reader to see the true form of things through its own medium. Hawthorne does not "idealize," though the word is a favorite expression in regard to him. All the talk of idealization, says Webber, is literary cant. Hawthorne has simply the faculty of transmuting the actual by presenting Nature to us in its most lovely aspects. " He is to the Present and the Future what Charles Lamb was to the Past." Here Webber compares Hawthorne with Lamb, to Hawthorne's at least ethical advantage. In any case:

It is certain that neither Lamb, nor any other Prose Writer has ever walked more critically that difficult and narrow line between the Natural and the Supernatural. . . . This is the highest accomplishment of a peculiar skill which all imaginative writers have emulated. Its perfect type is found in the Old Ballads. Walter Scott and Fouque have been masters; while in Poetry Coleridge has triumphed supremely in Cristobel.

Hawthorne has not equalled Scott in histrionic grandeur, nor *Undine* in grace and tenderness, nor *Cristobel* in mystery, says Webber, but "Young Goodman Brown" may, in his estimation, be compared with anything of this kind that has been done. Webber ends by saying that the true poet is the highest philosopher; it is as a true poet that he most profoundly respects Hawthorne. " Poetry is the music of Truth; and let it come through what medium it may, it is always musical while it is True! " He points to the deep poetry of " Rappaccini's Daughter."

Where out of Hell or Byron, will you find anything to compass the cold intellectual diabolism of the famous Doctor " Giacomo Rappaccini? " And when— certainly not in Byron!—will you find a sublime retribution visited upon that presumptuous thought, which dared the INEFFABLE and died!—which he there quietly gives.

We have given this article of Webber's some attention because it is a good, indeed an excellent, example of thoroughgoing romantic criticism, as well as because it gives an illustration (better than Hoffman's) of nationalistic aspirations in the field of literature. Romanticism in criticism differs somewhat from the attitude that we have labeled " sentimental appreciation," as will be obvious, though both spring from the same general current of thought. And moreover the article is an excellent appreciation, and a juster estimate of Hawthorne's higher powers than that presented by most of the critics of the other school. Webber does not linger over " Little Annie's Ramble " and he is not moved by the grand (if a little second-hand) allegory of " The Celestial Railroad." He quite rightly regards " Young Goodman Brown " as an example both of the original elements in Hawthorne's genius and of his mastery of his art.

The next article, found in *The New Englander*,[1] returns to a more usual attitude—or to an attitude, shall we say, more usual in New England. It was written by Samuel Dutton, an associate editor of the magazine and the celebrated pastor of New Haven's North Church. Dutton begins by saying that the works of Hawthorne, in his judgment, place him in the first rank of American writers, in the department of imaginative literature. He regrets that Hawthorne has been somewhat tainted by his sympathy for the " Concord sect " and the " Roxbury phalanx "; but observes Hawthorne's native good sense has evidently rescued him from " their loose doctrines, and their unsubstantial plans and theories." He continues:

---

[1] *New Englander* (5:56–69) January 1847. Nathaniel Hawthorne.

Mr. Hawthorne's style of writing greatly pleases us. While it is lively, graphic, and picturesque, and occasionally forcible, it is very natural and quiet. There is nothing strained, and no painfully manifest aim and effort to be brilliant and effective. We have become so wearied with these faults in modern writers, that it is really refreshing to read one who writes unambitiously and without this apparent labor—one who tells us his thoughts and emotions, without manifest consciousness of himself, and naturally, like the outbreaking of a fountain from the earth.

Dutton remarks on the simplicity of Hawthorne's style, which is, he says, like Addison's, Lamb's and Scott's, though not as majestic and rich as the latter. He admires the minuteness and charm of Hawthorne's observation and is, for this reason, particularly enchanted by " Buds and Bird-Voices " and " Snow-Flakes." His especial favorite is " The Celestial Railroad " which " surpasses all his other writings, and we were about to say, the writings of all but John Bunyan." Dutton points with appreciation to Hawthorne's humanity, and to his sympathy with the poor and humble. He objects to " The Gentle Boy " as unfair to the memory of the Puritan forefathers; and to " Young Goodman Brown " as too obscure. " An allegory with crutches is a poor affair. An illustration that needs to be illustrated, may well be spared." He ends by saying that Hawthorne is " quite equal " to Irving.

In November 1847 Edgar Allan Poe published in *Godey's* an article upon Hawthorne with the title *Tale Writing*.[1] It is longer and more elaborate than his previous essay, and, in some respects, it is strikingly different.

Poe begins by alluding to the passage in *Literati* in which he speaks of Hawthorne's reputation. He says that he was then right in citing Hawthorne as " the example, *par excellence,* in this country, of the privately-admired and publicly-unappreciated man of genius " but that Hawthorne's reputation has now begun a little to expand. (He refers to Webber's article as " a cordial and certainly full tribute.") Part of this " inappreciation," Poe continues, arose from the fact that he is neither a man of wealth nor a quack, but no small portion is attributable to the very marked idiosyncrasy of Hawthorne himself. For he is peculiar but not original. Here Poe pauses to distinguish

---

[1] *Godey's Lady's Book* (35:252–256) November 1847. Virginia Edition (13:141–151).

between peculiarity and originality. It is sometimes said, says Poe, that very original writers always fail in popularity. This is not true; for it is " the excitable, undisciplined and child-like popular mind " which feels the original most keenly. The criticism of the conservatives, of the hackneys and of the writers of the *North American Review* alone condemns originality. They demand quietude.

Opening their mouths with proper caution, they sigh forth the word " *Repose.*" And this is, indeed, the one thing they should be permitted to enjoy, if only upon the Christian principle of give and take.

If Hawthorne were really original, Poe repeats, he could not fail to make himself felt. But the fact is, he is not original in any sense. Those who speak of him as original mean that he differs from any other author of their acquaintance and their acquaintance does not extend to Tieck, " whose manner, in *some* of his works, is absolutely identical with that *habitual* to Hawthorne." Here Poe again returns to the discussion of originality. The element of literary originality, he says, is novelty; the element of its appreciation by the reader is the reader's sense of the new. Whatever gives him a new and, insomuch, a pleasureable emotion, he considers original; and whoever frequently gives him such emotion he considers an original writer. These points properly understood, Poe continues, it will be seen that the critic (unacquainted with Tieck) who reads a single piece of Hawthorne's may be justified in thinking him original; but the qualities which induce the sense of the new in the reader of one tale will fail to induce it when he reads a second or a third tale. After reading all his tales, the critic will abandon his first design of calling Hawthorne " original " and content himself with styling him " peculiar."

Poe would agree with the popular opinion that to be original is to be unpopular if he accepted the usual definition of originality, which limits the literary to the metaphysical quality by confounding originality with absolute novelty. Now, says Poe (turning his argument upon one of the central points of his critical theory), novelty of effect alone is worth consideration; and as a matter of fact pleasure, " the end of all fictitious compositions," is better attained by shunning rather than by seeking absolute novelty of combination. A reader is offended and his egoism is disturbed, by novelty; he is pleased by an apparent novelty (or true originality) which expresses his own half-formed fancies. " He feels and intensely enjoys the seeming novelty of the thought, enjoys it as really novel, as absolutely original with the writer —and himself."

There is a species of writing, Poe continues, which may be admitted as a lower degree of the true original. Its perusal occasions the reflection not " Here is an idea which I and the author have alone entertained " but " Here is a charmingly obvious fancy " or " Here is a thought which I am not sure has ever occurred to myself, but which, of course, has occurred to all the rest of the world." This composition, says Poe, is usually designated as " the natural." It is best exemplified, among English writers, in Addison, Irving and *Hawthorne*. The " ease " for which the *natural* style is often praised is, in Poe's opinion, no merit in particular. " The author who, after the manner of the ' North Americans ' is merely at *all* times *quiet,* is, of course, upon *most* occasions, merely silly or stupid. . . ."

Hawthorne's peculiarity, merely as peculiarity, says Poe, would be detrimental to his popularity; but the fact that he is peculiar at the worst of all possible points is fatal. This point is " the strain of allegory, which completely overwhelms the greater number of his subjects and which in some measure interferes with the direct conduct of absolutely all." Here Poe interjects his well known (and in more than one sense deservedly well known) opinion of allegory. There is scarcely one word to be said in defense of it, he says. The happiest allegory, as allegory, gives a most imperfectly satisfied sense of the writer's ingenuity in overcoming a difficulty we should have preferred his not having overcome. There is some justification for it only when the suggested meaning runs through the obvious one " in a *very* profound under-current " without interfering with the narrative.

Poe remarks that the obvious causes which have prevented Hawthorne's popularity do not suffice to condemn him " in the eyes of the few who belong properly to books, and to whom books, perhaps, do not quite so properly belong." From this point Poe launches into a long defense of the tale as a form of literature, repeating almost verbatim what he had said in his previous article—that the tale affords, because of its brevity and single effect, the fairest prose field for the exercise of the highest genius. Poe concludes by repeating that Hawthorne is peculiar and not original and that he is infinitely too fond of allegory; and by taking a fling at the Concord group and its supposed influence on Hawthorne.

Indeed his spirit of "metaphor run-mad" is clearly imbibed from the phalanx and phalanstery atmosphere in which he has been so long struggling for breath. He has not half the material for the exclusiveness of authorship that he possesses for its universality. He has the purest style, the finest taste, the most available scholarship, the most delicate humor, the most touching pathos, the most radiant imagination, the most consummate ingenuity; and with all these varied good qualities he has done well as a mystic. But is there any one of these qualities which should prevent his doing doubly well in a career of honest, upright, sensible, prehensible and comprehensible things? Let him mend his pen, get a bottle of visible ink, come out from the Old Manse, cut Mr. Alcott, hang (if possible) the editor of "The Dial," and throw out of the window to the pigs all his odd numbers of "The North American Review."

We need not comment in detail upon this article, for Poe is amply qualified to speak for himself, even in summary. We might refer, however, to an interesting article by Henry Belden [1] which deals with Poe's criticism of Hawthorne and which especially attempts to explain the differences of opinion between the *Graham's Magazine* article of 1842 and the *Godey's* article of 1846. It is Belden's opinion (an ingenious one) that Poe had seen the article in the *Foreign and Colonial Quarterly Review* in 1843 (or Duyckinck's quotation from it) which suggested that Hawthorne resembled Tieck; and that this suggestion had been reenforced in Poe's mind when he saw a translation from Tieck which appeared soon afterward in the *Democratic Review*. In other words, Belden says, Poe had been introduced to Tieck after he had written his article in *Graham's Magazine,* and had changed his mind in consequence. This is probable enough, though the theory is somewhat unsettled by an error of fact (which is shared apparently by a later researcher on the subject [2]). The first comparison with Tieck was not drawn by the *Foreign and Colonial Quarterly Review* in 1843 but by Duyckinck in his notice of April 1842 in *Arcturus.* That is to say, the comparison was suggested (and in a place where Poe, who saw everything in the periodical field, may

---

[1] Belden, H. M. Poe's Critique of Hawthorne. *Anglia* (23:376–404) 1910.
[2] See Randall Stewart's reference to an unpublished dissertation by H. A. Pochmann, *The Influence of the German Tale on the Short Stories of Irving, Hawthorne and Poe. American Notebooks,* p. 331.

easily have seen it) a month before Poe wrote his principal notice of
Twice-Told Tales. But the whole discussion is somewhat beside the
point. References to Tieck abound. The comparison suggested itself
independently to Duyckinck, to George James (if he is the author of
the article in the *Foreign and Colonial Review*) and to Chorley.
Lowell was to mention Tieck in *A Fable for Critics;* and Poe, who
was not entirely dependent upon chance references in periodicals for
his knowledge of current literature, may have thought of it himself.
The comparison was a very natural one. Tieck was the principal
author of distinction who had specialized in allegories in the form of
short stories; he had been translated by Carlyle; and he was a distinct
figure, or at least a prominent name, in the minds of persons interested
in literature. And as a matter of fact there is some resemblance between Tieck and Hawthorne, though of course the suggestion of influence (by Poe and by some modern scholars of the delving kind) is
ridiculous. Tieck's tales often sound, at least in translation, like
parodies of Hawthorne or like Hawthorne in his lowest and most
rigorously allegorical mood.

The principal difference between the articles of 1842 and of 1846 is
not, as Belden implies, the accusation of plagiarism. It lies in the
different subject matter of the two articles. In 1842 Poe was thinking mainly of the originality in literature and of its effect upon the
mind of the reader. In the first article he pays tribute to Hawthorne's mastery of the short story form; in the second, while incidentally repeating his former tribute, he casts about in his mind for an
explanation of Hawthorne's lack of popular appeal. The explanation
which he finds is (like many of his ratiocinations upon literature)
correct in essence and extravagant in detail. His well known tendency to discover plagiarism everywhere led him to pounce upon Tieck
as Hawthorne's original; but this accusation is really merely a detail,
an irrelevant detail, in his main argument.

Emerson had evidently been reading *Mosses from an Old Manse.*
We find in his journal for 1846 the succinct note: " Hawthorne in-
vites his readers too much into his study, opens the process before
them. As if the confectioner should say to his customers, ' Now, let
us make the cake.' " [1] This brief thought is constructive criticism of

---

[1] See his *Journals* (7:188).

a very refined sort; and it is doubly remarkable in being the only criticism we shall find, aside from Poe's, which touches, in any practical way, upon the art of the short story. Emerson meant, of course, that Hawthorne made an artistic error in sacrificing illusion by emphasizing the personal element in his tales. It is precisely what Poe should have said—what Poe would have said if his critical grasp had been as firm as it was keen, or if he had not been so easily led away from his subject by his own ideas—by considerations of plagiarism and of New England " mysticism," in this case. Emerson put his finger, with his own beautiful accuracy, upon a point which was a serious defect from Poe's point of view. Not from his own point of view, of course, because he regarded the writing of tales as a trifling occupation at best. But Poe took the importance of illusion for one of his cardinal critical principles, almost for his rule of life; and he should have seen, as Emerson saw, that the personal element in Hawthorne's manner was at least as grave an impediment to the production of the unified effect which he insisted upon, as the allegorical element.

In November *Blackwood's Magazine* published a notice of Wiley and Putnam's *Library of American Books* [1] which speaks briefly and scathingly of most of the offerings, but at more length and more favorably of *Mosses from an Old Manse.* In the general part of the article we find the note:

The " Mosses from an Old Manse " is occasionally written with an elegance of style which may almost bear comparison with that of Washington Irving; and though certainly it is inferior to the works of that author in taste and judgment, and whatever may be described as artistic talent, it exhibits deeper traces of thought and reflection.

Later the reviewer returns to Hawthorne, and remarks upon his contrast with Poe. Poe, he says, relies upon close detail and agglomeration of facts, while Hawthorne relies upon charm of style and play of thought and fancy. The most serious defect of Hawthorne's tales, he continues, is the presence of some palpable improbability. He points to " The Birth Mark " and " The Artist of the Beautiful " as containing, not nonsensical events, but nonsensical characters. The writer more especially approves of " those papers which we cannot

---

[1] *Blackwood's Magazine* (62:587-592) November 1847.

better describe as so many American *Spectators* of the year 1843—so much do they call to mind the style of essay in the days of Steele and Addison." He observes that American writers " frequently remind us of models of composition more antiquated than ourselves." While on one hand American authors have a tendency to snatch at originality at any cost, on the other hand they sometimes show an effort somewhat too apparent to be classical and correct. However, says the reviewer, this is a laudable effort. " We would merely observe that an effect is sometimes produced upon an English ear as if the writer belonged to a previous era of our literature, to an epoch when to produce smooth and well modulated sentences was something rarer and more valued than it is now." Hawthorne, continues the reviewer, reminds one pleasantly of Addison and Steele, though with some unfortunate lapses. He ends by recommending nearly all the pieces in the volume.

This article in *Blackwood's* is the last of the notices occasioned by the publication of *Mosses from an Old Manse,* but we might speak here (though somewhat out of place) of the most glowing tribute which the book received. This was in an article by Herman Melville which ran through two issues of the *Literary World* in August 1850.[1] Melville was then Hawthorne's neighbor and the two men had struck up a spontaneous friendship, an event which was rare enough in Hawthorne's career and especially rare in that his friend was a man of letters. For in general, as Woodberry points out, Hawthorne shrank from the society of men of his own profession. Melville published his article " Hawthorne and his Mosses " under the ingeniously deceptive heading " By a Virginian Spending the Summer in Vermont "; and no one at the time seems to have suspected his hand in it.

Melville begins by saying that he is compelled by love and duty to write of Hawthorne. " A man of deep and noble nature as seized me in this seclusion. His wild, witch-voice runs through me; or, in softer cadences, I seem to hear it in the songs of the hill-side birds that sing in the larch trees at my window." In his character of vacationing Virginian Melville goes on to explain that he has just read the *Mosses,* which were presented to him by " a mountain girl, a cousin of mine " to read in the haymow; and that he has been overcome by

---

[1] *Literary World* (7:125–127; 145–147) August 17, 24, 1850. Hawthorne and his Mosses, by a Virginian Spending the Summer in Vermont.

their charm. He speaks of the delicious restfulness of the volume, and of its humor.

What a wild moonlight of contemplative humor bathes that Old Manse!—the rich and rare distilment of a spicy and slowly-oozing heart. No rollicking rudeness, no gross fun fed on fat dinners, and bred in the lees of wine,—but a humor so spiritually gentle, so high, so deep, and yet so richly relishable, that it were hardly inappropriate in an angel. It is the very religion of mirth; for nothing so human but it may be advanced to that.

Here Melville pauses to celebrate various essays and tales in particular detail. The other side of Hawthorne's soul, he continues, is its " blackness, ten times black." This gloom is an inheritance from the old Calvinistic belief. " For in certain moods, no man can weigh this world without throwing in something, somehow like Original Sin, to strike the uneven balance." And no writer has employed this terrific thought with greater terror than Hawthorne. " He is immeasurably deeper than the plummet of the mere critic." Hawthorne must, says Melville, be understood by the heart; his greatness is revealed by intuition.

Melville goes on to draw a comparison between Shakespeare and Hawthorne. Shakespeare, he says, has been misunderstood by his admirers, who dream of him as " a mere man of Richard-the-Third humps and Macbeth daggers." What makes Shakespeare Shakespeare is " the occasional flash of intuitive truth in him—things which we feel to be so terrifically true, that it were but madness for any good man, in his own proper character, to utter, or even hint of them." Lear, tormented into desperation, speaks this madness of vital truth. Shakespeare's admirers, he continues, will stare to see his name and Hawthorne's upon the same page. Shakespeare has become a superstition, a fortieth article added to the thirty-nine articles of faith. " But what sort of a belief is this for an American, a man who is bound to carry republican progressiveness into Literature as well as into Life? " Melville adds:

Now I do not say that Nathaniel of Salem is greater than William of Avon, or as great. But the difference between the two men is by no means immeasurable. Not a very great deal more, and Nathaniel were verily William.

Shakespeare, he says, is bound to be surpassed upon one hemisphere or another, in a world where everything remains to be said. There follows an adjuration to America to cherish and glorify its own men of letters, and to follow its native bent. Melville refers to Irving with contempt as a writer who owes his success to avowed imitation. It is better, he says, to fail by originality than to succeed by imitation. "And we want no American Goldsmiths; nay, we want no American Miltons." He advises America to cherish and encourage Hawthorne in the present, rather than to admire him in the future, for he is "the American who up to the present day has shown the largest brain with the largest heart." Melville closes by saying that *Mosses,* which contains, unpretentiously set forth, some things "as deep as Dante" and "as sublime as Spenser," will ultimately be considered its author's masterpiece.[1]

This article is very characteristic of its author; though it is related in thought and style to other articles we have met. It recalls Hoffman and Webber in its unbounded aspirations toward a "truly national" literature; and it is much like Webber's essay in its determined romanticism. That is to say, Webber and Melville had both that bias of opinion, that ardor of temperament, which often saw "clouds, storms, effusions and relief" even where these elements were only moderately present. The article was pleasing to Hawthorne's friends. Sophia was charmed by it, for she saw her husband at last elevated to the position which she thought he deserved, namely, to an equality with Shakespeare; and Longfellow sent a copy of the article to Hawthorne with the note: "I have rarely seen a more appreciating and sympathizing critic; and though I do not endorse all he says about others, I do endorse all he says about you."[2]

In 1847 Rufus Griswold (who had previously obtained two poems from Hawthorne for his *Scenes in the Life of the Saviour*) published four of Hawthorne's pieces in his collection of *Prose Writers of America.*[3] The pieces were the "Rill from a Town Pump," "David Swan," "The Celestial Railroad," and an excerpt from "Buds and Bird Voices" called "Spring." In the introduction Griswold writes:

---

[1] However Melville, who seems to have read Hawthorne's writings in reverse chronological order, later said that *Twice-Told Tales* far exceeded the *Mosses.* See his letter to E. A. Duyckinck. Minnigerode, Meade. *Some Personal Letters of Herman Melville,* p. 56.

[2] See *Nathaniel Hawthorne and his Wife,* p. 384.

[3] Griswold, R. W. *Prose Writers of America.* New York 1847 (pp. 470–480).

Nathaniel Hawthorne has published some half dozen volumes of tales and romantic essays, various in character, but all marked with his peculiar and happy genius. He is "most musical, most melancholy." He controls his reader as the capricious air does the harp. The handkerchief, raised toward the eye to wipe away the blending moisture there, is checked at the lips, to suppress a smile, summoned by some touch of delicate and felicitous humour. He has the most unaffected simplicity and sincerity with the deepest insight into man's nature and the secrets of his action. His style is remarkable for elegance, clearness and ease, while it is imaginative and metaphysical; and his themes, chosen most frequently from the legends of our colonial age, though occasionally from those of a later period, or from the realm of allegory are not more than almost everything in his fanciful illustrations and quaint and beautiful philosophy. [*sic*] His Twice-Told Tales and Mosses from an Old Manse are the perfection of pensive, graceful, humorous writing, quite equal to the finest things of Diedrich Knickerbocker or Geoffrey Crayon, and superior to all else of a similar description in the English language.

In the preface to the selections Griswold gives a brief sketch of Hawthorne's life and character. In his critical comment he adds to what he has previously said the assertion that Hawthorne's style is "most poetical"; and he takes occasion silently to refute an adverse criticism by remarking that Hawthorne's good taste preserves him from presenting the conversations of the poor as full of grammatical blunders. "There is not in the world," he says proudly, "a large moral population which speaks its native language with a purity approaching that with which the English is spoken by the common people of New England." This anthology of Griswold's, which is really admirably composed and honestly representative of American literature, had a wide circulation both in America and abroad. Such knowledge of Hawthorne's life as existed in Europe seems to have been drawn entirely from Griswold's sketch.

We might well close this part of our study by citing the lines upon Hawthorne in *A Fable for Critics*.[1] They sum up excellently the opinions of at least one division of Hawthorne's critics, the members of "the school of sentimental appreciation,"—that is to say, Longfellow, Duyckinck, Peabody, Lowell himself. It will be noticed that the principal terms employed and comparisons made are those which we have heard before.

---

[1] [Lowell, James Russell] *A Fable for Critics.* 21 October 1848 (pp. 45–46).

There is Hawthorne, with genius so shrinking and rare
That you hardly at first see the strength that is there.
A frame so robust, with a nature so sweet,
So earnest, so graceful, so lithe and so fleet,
Is worth a descent from Olympus to meet;
'Tis as if a rough oak that for ages had stood,
With his gnarled bony branches, like ribs of the wood,
Should bloom, after cycles of struggle and scathe
With a single anemone trembly and rathe;
His strength is so tender, his mildness so meek,
That a suitable parallel sets one to seek,—
He's a John Bunyan Fouqué, a Puritan Tieck;
When Nature was shaping him, clay was not granted
For making so full-sized a man as she wanted,
So to fill out her model, a little she spared
From some finer-grained stuff for a woman prepared,
And she could not have hit a more excellent plan
For making him fully and perfectly man.

PART TWO

THE SCARLET LETTER, THE HOUSE OF THE SEVEN GABLES AND THE BLITHE-DALE ROMANCE

HAWTHORNE had almost ceased writing even while he was residing in the Old Manse; and when he returned to Salem as surveyor of the port, the malign influence of the custom-house, as well as some other disturbing circumstances, kept him altogether for a while from an occupation which had grown very hard. There are only four short pieces which belong to this period—" Main Street " which was published in 1849 in Elizabeth Peabody's *Æsthetic Papers,* " The Unpardonable Sin " (" Ethan Brand ") and " The Great Stone Face," which appeared in January 1850, the one in the *Boston Museum* and the other in Whittier's *National Era,* and lastly " The Snow Image " which was published at almost the same time in *The Memorial* and in the *International Magazine.* Hawthorne had almost exhausted his vein of short compositions, and, when he was engaged at all in literary effort, it was in a tentative and doubtful venture into another field.

James T. Fields, the publisher, visited Hawthorne in Salem in the winter that followed his dismissal from the custom-house and urged him to publish something new. He insisted that Hawthorne must have something ready to print. " Who would risk publishing anything for me, the most unpopular writer in America? " replied Hawthorne. " I would," said Fields, " and would start with an edition of two thousand copies of anything you write." Hawthorne, however, denied that he possessed anything; it was only as Fields was leaving that he ran after him and thrust into his hands the manuscript which contained the original version of *The Scarlet Letter.*[1] Even when Fields had enthusiastically consented to publish it and when the tale, expanded into something of the proportions of a novel, was al-

---

[1] Fields, J. T. *Yesterdays with Authors,* pp. 49–50.

ready in the press, Hawthorne remained dubious about its fate. He wrote to Horatio Bridge on the fourth of February, 1850:

> My book, the publisher tells me, will not be out before April. He speaks of it in tremendous terms of approbation. So does Mrs. Hawthorne, to whom I read the conclusion last night. It broke her heart and sent her to bed with a grievous headache, which I look upon as a triumphant success.
>
> Judging from its effect on her and the publisher, I may calculate on what bowlers call a ten strike. Yet I do not make any such calculation. Some portions of the book are powerfully written; but my writings do not, nor ever will, appeal to the broadest class of sympathies, and therefore will not obtain a very wide popularity.[1]

Hawthorne was quite wrong in thinking that the book would not sell. The first edition of *The Scarlet Letter* was exhausted in ten days, and a new edition was immediately printed. James Fields was an astute publisher and, though he could scarcely have anticipated the unprecedented demand for the book, he could reckon with some probability upon a profit. For Hawthorne, in spite of his often repeated assertion, was not the most unpopular writer in America.

As we have indicated, Hawthorne's reputation as a writer before 1850 was excellent; it lacked only the emphasis supplied by popularity. The great novel-reading public knew little of his writings, but the New England group (with the exception of Emerson) thought highly of his work, and it was favorably known to those of the elect who made a point of keeping in touch with what was being done in the field of American literature. That is, Hawthorne was known to the intellectual class (in which reviewers for magazines must necessarily be ranked) and his latest book did not fall on unploughed ground. As will be seen, nearly all the reviewers and commentators profess familiarity with his former writings.

The publishers saw to it that *The Scarlet Letter* was announced to the reading public as a book of unusual importance. In the *Literary World,* for instance, the following announcement appeared separately and in large type, running across the width of the page, in three successive issues:[2]

---

[1] Bridge, Horatio. *Personal Recollections of Nathaniel Hawthorne,* pp. 110–111.

[2] *Literary World* (6:211, 239, 288) March 2, 9, 16, 1850.

On Saturday, March 16th,
Will be published,
THE SCARLET LETTER: A ROMANCE
By Nathaniel Hawthorne
author of " Twice-Told Tales," " Mosses from
an Old Manse," etc., etc.
Ticknor, Reed and Fields,
135 Washington Street, Boston.

The book was accordingly published; and the first magazine to comment upon it was the *Literary World*. The voice is that of Duyckinck: [1]

> Mr. Hawthorne introduces his new story, the longest of all that he has yet published, and most worthy in this way to be called a romance, with one of those pleasant personal descriptions which are the most charming of his compositions, and of which we had so happy an example in the preface to his last collection, Mosses from an Old Manse. In these narratives everything seems to fall happily into its place. The style is simple and flowing, the observation accurate and acute; persons and things are represented in their minutest shades, and difficult traits of character presented with an instinct that art might be proud to imitate. They are, in fine, little cabinet pictures exquisitely painted. The readers of Twice Told Tales will know the pictures to which we allude. They have not, we are sure, forgotten Little Annie's Ramble or the Sights from a Steeple. . . .
>
> The Scarlet Letter is a psychological romance. The hardiest Mrs. Malaprop would never venture to call it a novel.[2] It is a tale of remorse, a study of character in which the human heart is anatomized carefully, elaborately and with striking poetic and dramatic power.

Duyckinck here summarizes the story and continues:

> But few as are these main incidents thus briefly told, the action of the story, or its passion, is " long, obscure, and infinite." It is a drama in which thoughts

---

1 *Literary World* (6:323–325) March 30, 1850.
2 On this distinction between a novel and a romance cf. *The Yale Literary Magazine* (19:253) June 1854. The undergraduate essayist there distinguishes the two forms: " There is," he says, " much the same difference between them as between the outlines of Dailey and of Lawrence, or between the rude caricatures of Hogarth and the shadowy paintings of a Venetian master. The one is a picture that must be true to every day life, but the other need not. While the one must confine itself to the natural, the other may employ the supernatural. The one is akin to history, the other to poetry."

are acts. The material has been thoroughly fused in the writer's mind, and springs forth an entire perfect creation. We know of no American tales except some of the early ones of Mr. Dana, which approach it in conscientious completeness. Nothing is slurred over, superfluous, or defective. . . .

Mr. Hawthorne has, in fine, shown extraordinary power in this volume, great feeling and discrimination, a subtle knowledge of character in its secret springs and outer manifestations. He blends, too, a delicate fancy with his metaphysical insight. We would instance the chapter toward the close, entitled " The Minister in a Maze," where the effects of a diabolic temptation are curiously depicted, or " The Minister's Vigil," the night scene in the pillory. The atmosphere of the piece also is perfect. It has the mystic element, the weird forest influences of the old Puritan discipline and era. Yet there is no affrightment which belongs purely to history, which has not its echo even in the unlike and perversely commonplace custom-house of Salem. Then for the moral. Though severe it is wholesome, and is a sounder piece of Puritan divinity than we have been of late accustomed to hear from the degenerate successors of Cotton Mather. We hardly know another writer who has lived so much among the new school who would have handled this delicate subject without an infusion of George Sand. The spirit of his old Puritan ancestors, to whom he refers in his preface, lives in Nathaniel Hawthorne.

We will not mar the integrity of the Scarlet Letter by quoting detached passages. Its simple and perfect unity forbids this. Hardly will the introductory sketch bear this treatment without exposing the writer to false impressions, but as evidence of the possession of a style faithfully and humorously reflective of the scenes of the passing hour, which we earnestly wish he may pursue in future volumes, we may give one or two separable sketches.

Duyckinck then gives a number of extracts from the preface; and ends his article with the conclusion: " Our literature has given to the world no truer product of the American soil, though of a peculiar culture, than Nathaniel Hawthorne."

We have quoted the *Literary World's* review almost complete because it says in sum what several subsequent reviewers also say.

Two days later, the *New York Daily Tribune* [1] published an article by George Ripley, the founder of Brook Farm and the advocate of many another idealistic cause. He had then recently come to fill the literary department of the *Tribune,* succeeding that other eminent Transcendentalist, Margaret Fuller. He describes the book and re-

---

[1] The *New York Daily Tribune* (p. 2, supp.) April 1, 1850.

marks that its subject eminently suits Hawthorne's peculiar genius; and then proceeds to compare him with Poe, a comparison that for some reason was rarely made by American critics. Hawthorne enchants the reader, he says, with an art similar to Poe's, but his tragedies " are always motived with wonderful insight and skill to which the intellect of Poe was a stranger." Thus the terror of his supernatural effects is lightened and made bearable by humanity. He adds that *The Scarlet Letter* is the greatest production of the author, and that while the querulous tone of the introduction is objectionable, it may be forgiven to the sensitiveness of a poet.

The May issue of *Graham's Magazine*,[1] where Hawthorne's good friend Edwin Percy Whipple was for the time in charge of the literary department, says:

> In this beautiful and touching romance Hawthorne has produced something really worthy of the fine and deep genius which lies within him. . . . In the "Scarlet Letter" we have a complete work, evincing a true artist's certainty of touch and expression in the exhibition of characters and events, and a keen-sighted vision into the essence and purpose of spiritual laws. There is a profound philosophy underlying the story which will escape many of the readers whose attention is engrossed by the narrative.
>
> The book is prefaced by some fifty pages of autobiographical matter, relating to the author, his native city of Salem and the Custom House, from which he was once ousted by the Whigs. These pages, instinct with the vital spirit of humor, show how rich and exhaustless a fountain of mirth Hawthorne has at his command. The whole representation has the dreamy yet distinct remoteness of the purely comic ideal.

The reviewer remarks that the book is uniformly and concentratedly gloomy; then he adds:

> If there be, however, a comparative lack of relief to the painful emotion which the novel excites, owing to the intensity with which the author concentrates attention on the working of dark passions, it must be confessed that the moral purpose of the book is made more definite by this very deficiency. The most abandoned libertine could not read this volume without being thrilled into something like virtuous resolution, and the ' roué ' would find that the deep-seeing eye of the novelist had mastered the whole philosophy of guilt of which practical roués are but childish disciples. To another class of readers, those who have theories of seduction and adultery modeled after the French school of novelists,

---

[1] *Graham's Magazine* (36:345–346) May 1850.

and to whom [sic] libertinism is of the brain, the volume may afford matter for very instructive and edifying contemplation; for, in truth, Hawthorne, in the Scarlet Letter, has utterly undermined the whole philosophy on which the French novels rest, by seeing farther and deeper into the essence back of conventional and moral laws; and he has given the results of his insight, not in disquisitions and criticisms, but in representations more powerful even than those of Sue, Dumas, or George Sand. He has made the guilty parties end, not as his own fancy, or his own benevolent sympathies might dictate, but as the spiritual laws, lying back of all persons, dictated to him. . . .

Whipple concludes:

In his next work, we hope to have a romance equal to the Scarlet Letter in pathos and power, but more relieved by touches of that beautiful and peculiar humor, so serene and searching, in which he excels almost all living writers.

The three foregoing reviews may stand as representative of the immediate impression made by The Scarlet Letter. On the whole, their tone might have been anticipated. Any American work of merit might reasonably hope for a favorable opinion from the Literary World or from Graham's Magazine. The reviews in both were seldom condemnatory; they inclined to " puffery " rather than to severity. Any work which described a distinctly American scene, which had a distinctly American tone, might be sure of a welcome. That all three reviewers should commend Hawthorne's style and his method of dealing with the supernatural, is quite natural; both elements are excellent by any standard of criticism, and they fell in with taste of the period. What might also be expected, in view of the inclinations of the day, is the implied preference for the introductory sketch. Hawthorne himself had expected this. In the letter to Bridge which has been quoted previously he wrote: " There is an introduction to this book giving a sketch of my custom-house life, with an imaginative touch here and there, which may, perhaps, be more widely attractive than the main narrative. The latter lacks sunshine, etc." [1]

The general tenor of these three reviews is quite usual. There is one important element in all three, however, which could scarcely have been expected. They insist on the fact that Hawthorne has vindicated " conventional and moral laws "; Whipple becomes enthusiastic in his recommendation of Hawthorne's moral teaching. As a matter of fact,

---

[1] Personal Recollections of Nathaniel Hawthorne, p. 111.

Hawthorne does not vindicate conventional morality. Hester Prynne is nowhere represented as repenting of her sin; at the end of the stòry it is only chance and Dimmesdale's exhaustion which prevents the lovers from escaping and renewing their former relations. Chillingworth, who, from the point of view of conventional morality, is the innocent and injured person, is represented as the real criminal, the person upon whom the initial responsibility rests. Dimmesdale, whose convictions are conventional and Calvinistic, is represented as weak and unmanly. It is true that Hawthorne nowhere explicitly states (as he does later in *The Marble Faun*) that sin is important, even necessary for the development of the human soul; he leaves the reader, in this case, to infer the moral from the story and to make out the symbolism as best he may. Yet Hawthorne does not attempt to conceal his point; the reviewers' blindness can only be accounted for by the fact that the story is a gloomy one. They may have supposed that since sin was treated darkly, it must have been treated in an orthodox manner. There is no touch of licentiousness in the story; in this respect, the reviewers point out, unlike George Sand—a writer whose works, we learn elsewhere, were enjoying a dangerous popularity among novel readers in America.[1]

The next notice of *The Scarlet Letter* is an English one; it was given a prominent place in an issue in which *In Memoriam* was also reviewed. Henry Chorley in the *Anthenaeum* (its authoritative English voice, one may fancy, rising above the more uncertain voices of the American journals) pronounces his verdict:[2]

This is a most powerful but painful story. Mr. Hawthorne must be well known to our readers as a favourite with the *Athenaeum*. We rate him as among the most original and peculiar writers of American fiction. There is in his works a mixture of Puritan reserve and wild imagination, of passion and description, of the allegorical and the real, which some will fail to understand and others will reject—but which, to ourselves, is fascinating, and which entitles him to be placed on a level with Brockden Brown and the author of Rip Van Winkle. The "Scarlet Letter" will increase his reputation with those who do not shrink from the invention of the tale; but this, as we have said, is more than ordinarily painful.

---

[1] Cf. Jones, H. M. American Comment on George Sand 1837–1848. *American Literature* (3:389–407) January, 1932. We shall hear more of George Sand in future reviews.

[2] *Athenaeum* (no. 1181: p. 634) June 15, 1850.

The reviewer continues with a discussion of the suitability of the subject for artistic treatment:

> We are by no means satisfied that passions and tragedies like these are the legitimate subjects for fiction; we are satisfied that novels such as "Adam Blair" and plays such as "The Stranger" may be justly charged with attracting more persons than they warn by their excitement. But if Sin and Sorrow in their most fearful forms are to be represented in any work of art they have rarely been presented with loftier severity, purity, and sympathy than in Mr. Hawthorne's "Scarlet Letter."

Even Chorley, it may be seen, although troubled with a faint doubt about the material itself, does not doubt the essential morality of Hawthorne's story. The reference to *Adam Blair* is interesting; for Lockhart's novel was the subject of much discussion in England at that day, and the general verdict was on the whole condemnatory. Henry James compares the two in his study of Hawthorne with his customary fine perception; and points out incidentally that, while the treatment of *Adam Blair* is far more realistic than that of *The Scarlet Letter,* it is nevertheless more conventional in its thought.

This review may be regarded as placing Hawthorne quite accurately in the position to which he fell heir on the publication of *The Scarlet Letter.* For Americans and those of the English who were interested in things American, Hawthorne was now among the more important American writers. *The Scarlet Letter,* with its extraordinary sale, had set the seal upon an already promising reputation. The best evidence of its establishment in the mind of the public is the fact that the comments which one now hears are not reviews but attacks. We find three attacks and one elaborate defense.

Anne W. Abbott, writing a review for the *North American Review* of July,[1] is the first to indicate dissatisfaction with the moral import of the book. She begins with a discussion and résumé of the preface, and continues:

> We confess that, to our individual taste, this naughty chapter is more piquant than anything in the book; the style is racy and pungent, not elaborately written, but stimulating the reader's attention agreeably by original terms of expression and in unhackneyed combinations of words, falling naturally into their places, as if of their own accord, and not obtained by far seeking and impress-

---

[1] *North American Review* (71:135–148) July 1850.

ment into service. . . . The delineation of wharf scenery and of the Custom House, with their appropriate figures and personages, are worthy of the pen of Dickens; and really so far as the style is concerned, Mr. Hawthorne has no reason to thank us for the compliment; he has the finer touch, if not the more genial feeling, of the two.

Miss Abbott comments upon the magical effect of Hawthorne's style and its ability to take the reader out of the ordinary world; then adds: " His imagination has sometimes taken him fairly off his feet, insomuch that he seems to doubt if there be any firm ground at all,— if we may judge from such mist born ideas as the following." She then quotes the passage on Roger Chillingworth in which Hawthorne speculates whether love and hate are not the same thing at bottom. Later in the article she says:

Hester at first sight, strongly excites our pity, for she suffers like an immortal being; and our interest in her continues only while we have hope for her soul, that its baptism of tears will reclaim it from the foul stain that has been cast upon it. We see her humble, meek, self-denying, charitable, and heart-wrung with anxiety for the moral welfare of her wayward child. But anon her humility catches a new tint, and we find it pride; and so a vague unreality steals by over all her most humanizing traits—we lose our confidence in all—and finally, like Undine she disappoints us, and shows the dream-land origin and nature, when we were looking to behold a Christian.

Miss Abbott thinks Dimmesdale and Chillingworth equally unconvincing; of Pearl she says, however, that Hawthorne unconsciously draws a better picture than he intended. She praises Hawthorne's descriptive powers and the charm of his style, charming " especially in this day, when fear of triteness drives some writers (even those who might otherwise avoid the reproach) to adopt an abrupt and dislocated style," and concludes: " One cannot but wonder by the way that the master of such a wizard power over language as Mr. Hawthorne manifests should not choose a less revolting subject than this of the Scarlet Letter, to which fine writing seems as inappropraite as fine embroidery. The ugliness of pollution and vice is no more relieved by it than the gloom of the prison is by the rose tree at its door. There are some palliative expressions used which cannot, even as a matter of taste, be approved."

In the *Massachusetts Quarterly Review* for September [1] George Bailey Loring published a long and eloquent defense of *The Scarlet Letter*. The *Massachusetts Quarterly Review* (conducted by Theodore Parker) was at the moment the Transcendental organ. It was, in fact, the successor to the *Dial,* though chiefly devoted to political questions: " the *Dial* with a beard," as some one called it. Loring, as might be expected from the principles of the group in general, was enthusiastic over Hawthorne's freedom of mind. He says:

> It seems useless now to speak of his humor, subtle and delicate as Charles Lamb's; of his pathos, deep as Richter's, of his penetration into the human heart, clearer than that of Goldsmith or Crabbe, of his apt and telling words which Pope might have envied, of his descriptions, graphic as Scott's or Dickens'.

He remarks that Hawthorne never troubles himself with the surroundings of life, that his interest is in giving a picture of " the motive heart of man." He continues:

> In no work of his is this characteristic more strikingly visible than in " the *Scarlet Letter*"; and in no work has he presented so clear and perfect an image of himself, as a speculative philosopher, an ethical thinker, a living man. Perhaps he verges strongly upon the supernatural, in the minds of those who recognize nothing but the corporeal existence of human life. But man's nature is by birth supernatural; and the deep mystery which lies beneath all his actions is far beyond the reach of any mystical vision that ever lent its airy shape to the creations of the most intense dreamer.

Loring continues with the observation that we should be thankful for Hawthorne's custom-house experience, since it gave Hawthorne opportunity for such observation; " and we are reminded," he proceeds, " of the strong human groups of Tenier and Poussin, as we read the graphic picture of those old custom-house attachés from the pen of Hawthorne." He then plunges again into his thesis, which he prefaces with a long and admirable analysis of the effects of sin on the two protagonists of the story. Sin and temptation, he says, have a redeeming power; artificial—that is, untried—virtue is useless. Of Hester he says:

---

[1] *Massachusetts Quarterly Review* (3:484–500) September 1850.

In casting her out, the world had torn from her all the support of its dogmatic teachings, with which it sustains its disciples in their inevitable sufferings, and had compelled her to rely upon that great religious truth which bows instinctively around a life of agony, with its daring freedom. How far behind her in moral and religious excellence was the accredited religious teacher, who was her companion in guilt.

Of Hester's love he says:

We dare not call this a wicked perversity, which brought its possessor into that state of strong and fiery resolution and elevation, which enabled her to raise her lover from his craven sense of guilt into a solemn devotion to his better nature. . . . This bore her though her trial; and this, at that glowing hour when both rose above the weight which bowed them down, tore the scarlet letter from her breast and made her young and pure again. The ecstasy of Murillo's conception, the calm solemn maternity of Raphael's madonnas, the sterling wealth of beauty in Titian's Magdalens, and the appealing and teaching heart of woman, in all these, come crowding before us, as we rise with Hester to this holy exaltation.

He ends:

There is a sweeping belief that vice stands at one pale and virtue at the other, which the deep trials of life eradicate. There is a want of sympathy for the erring, and an ignorant closing of the heart against those whose entrance would enlarge and beautify and warm our souls, which the experience of our own temptation would remove.

This is espousing Hawthorne's cause with a vengeance. Hawthorne himself never went so far in commending his theories; he states them, if he states them at all, with a lightly sceptical air, as if willing to recall them at any opportunity. Loring's article, however, is a very able analysis of the ethical problem implicit in *The Scarlet Letter*. It represents the point of view of a very small group; for the *Massachusetts Quarterly Review* probably had an audience not much larger than that of the *Dial*. It was conducted by a group of enthusiasts whose theories were repugnant to the general public; [1] Loring himself was not then a friend of Hawthorne's but his opinions may fairly represent those of the more intellectual members of Haw-

---

[1] For a common opinion of the New England group cf. A. C. Coxe's article in the *Church Review* for January, 1851, quoted below.

thorne's acquaintance. Even Brownson (whose article comes next by date) individualist that he was, and, in a sense, honorary member of the New England group, represents a more usual point of view.

In the October issue of Brownson's Review [1] Orestes Augustus Brownson takes up the attack on The Scarlet Letter. He writes:

Mr. Hawthorne is a writer endowed with a large share of genius, and in the species of literature he cultivates has no rival in this country, unless it be Washington Irving. . . . The work before us is the largest and most elaborate of the romances he has yet published, and no one can read half a dozen pages of it without feeling that none but a man of true genius and a highly cultivated mind could have written it. It is a work of rare, we may say, of fearful power, and to a great body of our countrymen who have no well defined religious belief, and no fixed principles of virtue, it will be deeply interesting and highly pleasing.

We have neither the space nor the inclination to attempt an analysis of Mr. Hawthorne's genius, after the manner of the fashionable criticism of the day. Mere literature for its own sake we do not prize, and we are more disposed to analyze an author's work than the author himself. Men are not for us mere psychological phenomena, to be studied, classed, labelled. They are moral and accountable beings, and we look only to the moral and religious effect of their works. Genius perverted, or employed in perverting others, has no charms for us, and we turn away from it with sorrow and disgust. God gave us our faculties to be employed in his service, and in that of our fellow creatures for his sake, and our only legitimate office as critics is to inquire, when a book is sent us for review, if its author in producing it has so employed them.

Having stated his position as a reviewer—a position in which the ardor of a new convert to Catholicism is clearly apparent—Brownson continues:

There is an unsound state of public morals when the novelist is permitted, without a scorching rebuke, to select such crimes, and to invest them with all the fascinations of genius, and all the claims of a highly polished style. In a moral community such crimes are spoken of as rarely as possible, and when spoken of at all, it is always in terms which render them loathsome, and repel the imagination.

Brownson continues with the observation that neither of the two criminals repented of their crime; Hester suffers from regret and her disgrace, Dimmesdale from his hypocrisy and cowardice. The sin it-

---

[1] Brownson's Review (7:528–532), October 1850.

self, he says, does not seem to have been regarded as sinful; the attempted excuse (that Hester did not love her husband) only darkens the offense; a woman is divinely commanded to love her husband. He concludes:

> The Christian who reads the *Scarlet Letter* cannot fail to perceive that the author is wholly ignorant of Christian asceticism, and that the highest principle of action he recognizes is pride. In both criminals, the long and intense agony they are represented as suffering springs not from remorse, from the consciousness of having offended God, but mainly from the feeling that they have failed to maintain the integrity of their characters. . . .
>
> As a picture of the old Puritans, taken from the position of a moderate transcendentalist and liberal of the modern school, the work has its merits; but as little as we sympathize with those stern old Popery-haters, we do not regard the picture as at all just. We should commend where the author condemns and condemn where he commends. Their treatment of the adulterers was far more Christian than his ridicule of it. But enough of faultfinding, and as we have no praise, except what we have given, to offer, we close this brief notice.

Although Brownson makes something of a parade of his Catholic standards, they are exactly those of any orthodox churchman, Catholic or Protestant. The Rev. Coxe, whose article follows next by date speaks, rather more fervently, in almost the same terms.

In the *Church Review,* the most important of the Protestant Episcopal magazines, appeared in January, 1851, an article called "The Writings of Hawthorne." [1] Its writer, Arthur Cleveland Coxe, was a poet of some reputation, composer of several well-known volumes of sacred poetry and prolific author of articles. He introduces his subject by a disquisition on reviewing in general. Reviews in American magazines, he says, are usually written either for favor or for spite. They have no substance. It is for this reason that English magazines are much more highly respected than American magazines. Though he has himself none of the qualifications of the ideal reviewer, he will take up Hawthorne's works impartially with the object of showing Hawthorne the effects that his writings are producing "on a large, but quiet portion of the community." He will be quite impartial, he repeats; then he qualifies his statement:

---

[1] *Church Review* (3:489–511) January 1851. A partial reprint of the article is found in *Notorious Literary Attacks,* A. Mordell, New York 1926.

True we must own to a little prejudice against him, as a conspicuous member of the Bay School, but in counterpoise, we must put in a profession of a special feeling in his favor, as at all events one of the best of them, the very Irving of Down-East. He is one of the few Bays whose freest egotism seldom moves our disgust, and whom we are, in truth, disposed to thank for gossiping at random about himself and friends, as if everyone knew both himself and them, and were anxiously watching them with telescopes and lorgnettes.

Hawthorne's humorously expressed dismay at finding his name and talents unknown in the custom-house, is another proof (if proof were needed) of the insufferable sense of self-importance that pervades the whole group. " The fact is, a Bay-writer is too commonly affected with a painful sense of literary consequence; he lives among imaginary Boswells; he feels that eating, drinking, sleeping and snoring with him are a virtual biography." Speaking of Hawthorne's complaint, in the character of M. de l'Aubepine, that he stands between the popular and the transcendental schools and thus finds himself without an audience, Coxe writes:

Pooh, pooh! Mr. Hawthorne, are you in earnest or are you not? If not— why, in the name of sense, stand whining about Mons. de l'Aubepine's unpopularity, when you know that Hawthorne's books are fairly thumbed to pieces by the readers of all circulating libraries, and that everyone is disposed to like them and to buy them; if you are, pray throw away your transcendentalism and your sympathetic ink, your refinement and your remoteness, your circle and your clique, and come down to flesh and blood, and live, and act, and talk like other men, and we assure you, you have talents that will take care of themselves. . . . In our opinion, a little less starch and cambric and a little more bone and sinew would be the thing for many a fellow in the Bay metropolis who is always " dying of a rose in aromatic pain "; and we never hear a really gifted man talking in this vein of Mons. de l'Aubepine, without longing to make so bold as to ask him to a bit of roast beef and a bottle of brown stout, in a plain, family way, with the benevolent idea of invigorating his constitution in time to prevent the process of evaporative dissolution.

He is very sorry, continues Coxe, to find that Hawthorne is afflicted with the " provinciality " of the Bay School; for he had been very much taken with Hawthorne, on first impression, when he read " The Celestial Railroad " in a newspaper. " The Celestial Railroad," he says, is one of the cleverest, best sustained and ingenious specimens of satire in our language. Hawthorne may well be compared with Irving, he proceeds. Irving is the better artist; but if Hawthorne had " the taste and discrimination and something more of the instinctive delicacy " of Irving, there would be little distinction between them. This opinion of Hawthorne's work was confirmed, he adds, by a " European Periodical " of several years before.[1]

Coxe now plunges into the principal subject of his article: an indignant reprobation of Hawthorne's latest work. He sees with horror the possibilities of a flood of imitations of George Sand in America; and he is the more concerned in this particular case in that Hawthorne's work might easily be the vehicle of deep suggestion and pure amusement. He hopes that the success of this venture will not encourage Hawthorne to select similar themes for his next works. The Puritan period, he points out, is full of themes for romance: why should Hawthorne have chosen this subject?

Is it, in short, because a running undercurrent of filth has become as requisite to a romance, as death in the fifth act of a tragedy? Is the French era actually begun in our literature? And is the flesh, as well as the world and the devil, to be henceforth dished up in fashionable novels, and discussed at parties, by spinsters and their beaux, with as unconcealed a relish as they give to the vanilla in their ice cream?

To illustrate the deleterious effect of *The Scarlet Letter* Coxe relates an incident which had occurred in Maine the previous summer. He was travelling in a stagecoach with a party of schoolgirls; and, pretending to be asleep, he listened to their conversation, which happened to fall on the subject of literature. The young ladies agreed that Scott and Irving were charming writers, they quoted Longfellow, and at last they came to Hawthorne:

We expected a quotation from the " Celestial Railroad," for we were travelling at a rate which naturally raised the era of railroads in one's estimation by the rule of contrary; but no—the girls went straight to " the Scarlet Letter." We soon discovered that one Hester Prynne was the heroine, and that she had been made to stand on a pillory, as, indeed, her surname might have led us to anticipate. We discovered that there was a mysterious little child in the question, that she was a sweet little darling, and that her " sweet, pretty little name " was " Pearl." We discovered that mother and child had a meeting, in a wood, with a very fascinating young preacher, and that there was a hateful

---

[1] The " European Periodical " was *Blackwood's* of November 1847.

creature named Chillingworth who persecuted the said preacher, very persever-ingly. Finally, it appeared that Hester Prynne was, in fact, Mrs. Hester Chilling-worth, and that the hateful old creature aforesaid had a very natural dislike to the degradation of his spouse, and quite as natural a hatred of the wolf in sheep's clothing who had wrought her ruin. All this leaked out in conversation, little by little, on the hypothesis of our protracted somnolency. There was a very gradual approximation to the point, till one inquired—" didn't you think, from the first, that he was the one? " A modest looking creature, who evidently had not read the story, artlessly inquired—" what one? "—and then there was a titter at the child's simplicity, in the midst of which we ventured to be quite awake, and to discover by the scarlet blush that began to circulate, that the young ladies were not unconscious to themselves that reading " the Scarlet Let-ter " was a thing to be ashamed of. These school girls had, in fact, done injury to their young sense of delicacy, by devouring such a dirty story; and after talk-ing about it before folk, inadvertently, they had enough of Mother Eve in them to know that they were ridiculous and that shame was their best retreat.

Coxe admits that *The Scarlet Letter* is not coarse in detail or indecent in phraseology; its perfectly chaste diction, however, is so arranged as to suggest sympathy with the criminals and a wish that they may escape and renew their crime in another land. *The Vicar of Wakefield* is occasionally coarse in its language, but it is coarsely virtuous. *The Scarlet Letter* is delicately immoral. Shelley himself never imagined a more dissolute conversation than that between Hester and Dimmesdale in which Hester cries that their love had a consecration of its own. As for the feminist doctrines that Hester seems to recommend at the end of the story, they must be regarded with horror by all who love women. The very suggestion of another mode of life for women than that of her God given sphere is an insult and a degradation.

Coxe concludes his article as he began it. It is only an earnest wish for Mr. Hawthorne's future, he repeats, that has led to a criticism so little to his taste.

We have given a good deal of attention to Coxe's article because it is, for several reasons, significant. In the first place, the article, unlike most of the material with which we are dealing, has a certain intrinsic value; the force of the writer's conviction lent weight to his style and gave point to his malice. The essay, departing as it does from the usual half-meaningless phrases of the reviews, is impressive;

and it is, besides, almost famous, in that some of its salient sentences have been often quoted.

Brownson and Coxe are the only writers who attack *The Scarlet Letter* directly on the point of morals. Even Miss Abbott bases her adverse criticism on the grounds of art: Hester's lack of Christian principles, she says, makes her *unreal;* the palliative expressions used offend good taste. Brownson and Coxe disclaim any interest in art, except as it promotes the moral welfare of the reader; they are both concerned with preserving the purity of literature. Coxe is more important because he is more particular. Brownson writes in general terms; Coxe, with exactly the same convictions in mind, is admirably illustrative.

It is in Coxe that one obtains a concrete statement of one important phase of the nationalistic spirit that pervaded the criticism of the day: the demand that American writing should be, not only individual, but pure. This demand was not local to New England and cannot be regarded as a specific inheritance from the old Puritans, who were themselves in fact quite sufficiently outspoken. It was a national phenomenon and it arose naturally from a conjunction of the taste of the age with those noble hopes for the future of the republic which were then expressed, and felt, by all good Americans. It was understood that European writers, and especially French writers, had a certain license to deal with dubious subjects; but it was important that Americans should not read them and, above all, should not imitate them. The spread of cheap editions of Eugene Sue and George Sand was to be deplored; that any American writer of repute should follow them, however far off, was unthinkable. The necessity of unimpeachable morals in any work of art was so well understood that the subject was seldom mentioned. A glance at the literature of the time, at the innumerable female writers, even at the eminent writers whose works have survived, will confirm the prevalence of this tacit agreement. Whitman's *Leaves of Grass,* which appeared five years after this date, was so singular a violation of it, that it was ignored as the work of a madman. In Coxe's article we get a hint that the success of *The Scarlet Letter* was obtained partly in spite of, and partly because of, this national literary standard.

In Coxe's sketch of the young ladies of the stagecoach we obtain our only representation of the manner in which *The Scarlet Letter* affected the unintellectual class of novel readers—the class which was, after all, responsible for the sale of the book. The professional reviewers found it suitable to judge the book from an intellectual point of view—that is to say, they criticize it as a work of art. Coxe's schoolgirls, like Coxe himself, have no concern with *The Scarlet Letter* as art. They regarded it as a story; and the interest they felt in it may be regarded as typical. The fact that the story was by an American author of reputation automatically placed it within the prescribed limits of young ladies' readings; they could not read—or at least, could not so publicly acknowledge their reading of —George Sand. And yet they were conscious that the story was rather more exciting than those to which they had been accustomed. The blush which Coxe approved and the titter which he did not approve are both acknowledgments that *The Scarlet Letter* possessed, in its subject matter, a certain unusual fascination.

One may deduce from Coxe's incident that *The Scarlet Letter* had, in a mild way, a *succès de scandale*. The book was, of course, not popularly regarded as scandalous. The strict propriety of the diction and the fact that its unconventionality was so veiled as to escape all but such acute observers as Loring, Brownson, and Coxe, were sufficient to give it an air of decorum. When the *Literary World*, the *Tribune, Graham's* and the *Anthenaeum* unanimously agreed that *The Scarlet Letter* was a piece of authentic Puritan morality, one may be sure that the general public considered it a very moral book. The novelty of its subject, however, and the concentration on the theme of sin, must have had something to do with its popular success; in an age in which Scott still reigned supreme, *The Scarlet Letter* had something of a morbid fascination.

The last four articles that we have considered (Miss Abbott's, Loring's, Brownson's, and Coxe's) bear testimony to the fact that *The Scarlet Letter* was by that time established in the public consciousness. The first articles that we quoted were reviews—commendatory, to be sure. The last articles obviously indicate that the writers had read, or reread, *The Scarlet Letter* in the face of public pressure. The fact that there are three attacks, as we have said before, reveals in itself that the book had been highly praised. Loring's comment is too admiring wholly to be trusted. The enthusiasm of the writer carries him, as he himself implies, to an expression of praise far beyond that which might be expected of the casual reader. The admissions wrung from the enemies of the book are of more importance. Brownson and Coxe both mention Hawthorne and Irving in one breath. They scarcely qualify their admissions that Hawthorne is on the same plane as that of the most distinguished man of letters in America. Coxe implies that it is on the score of delicacy and moral fitness alone that Irving surpasses Hawthorne; Brownson merely says that Hawthorne has no rival, unless it be Washington Irving. They both profess horror that so eminent a talent should be so ignobly employed.

One may see that Hawthorne has taken a sudden leap in public estimation. Before the appearance of *The Scarlet Letter* Hawthorne was one among a crowd of American writers. His tales were read with appreciation by an isolated group, and, without any especial appreciation, by the subscribers to the magazines in which his tales appeared. Within the space of a few months he had come to be reckoned confidently among the very brightest stars of the literary heavens. The attacks of Brownson and Coxe, significant as they are for our purposes, had little effect on the reputation of the book. The moral issue did not rise to the importance of a public controversy. Coxe's article is not notorious in the sense that Mr. Mordell seems to imply when he includes it in a book called *Notorious Literary Attacks.* His public (the subscribers to the *Church Review*) was fairly limited; Brownson's public was even more limited. As we shall see from the first review of *The House of the Seven Gables,* their comments apparently did not disturb the calm surface of the reviewer's mind by so much as a ripple.

A private opinion which expressed the thoughts of a large group of Hawthorne's admirers is found in a letter of George Hillard, who was, it should be remembered, the friend who had solved Hawthorne's difficulties in the black days following his dismissal from the custom-house by taking up a subscription and presenting it to him, with the graceful excuse that it was owing to him as a recompense for his contribution to American letters. Hillard says: [1]

You have written a most remarkable book; in point of literary talent, beyond all your previous efforts; a book full of tragic power, nice observation, delicate

---

[1] See *Memories of Hawthorne,* pp. 121–122.

tact, and a rare knowledge of the human heart. I think it will take a place in our literature among the highest efforts of what may be called the Tragic Muse of Fiction. . . . For my own taste, I could wish that you would dwell more in the sun, and converse more with cheerful thoughts and lightsome images, and expand into a story the spirit of the Town Pump.

We should also note here Oliver Wendell Holmes' lines upon *The Scarlet Letter*.[1] They occurred originally in a long poem called " Astraea, or the Balance of Illusions " delivered before the Yale Phi Beta Kappa Society. In the passage which mentions *The Scarlet Letter* Holmes is speaking of the different pleasures provided by his dull old books and by the " damp offspring of the modern press " :

> Not less I love each dull familiar face
> No less should miss it from the appointed place.
> I snatch the book, along whose burning leaves,
> His scarlet web our wild romancer weaves.
> Yet while proud Hester's fiery pangs I share,
> My old Magnalia must be standing there!

These lines were frequently quoted, probably because the phrases admirably express the attitude of many of the book's first readers.

Hawthorne himself, though he had been wrong in anticipating failure for *The Scarlet Letter,* had been right in one detail of his supposition. " There is an introduction to this tale," he wrote in the letter to Bridge which we have quoted before, " giving a sketch of my custom-house life, with an imaginative touch here and there, which may, perhaps, be more widely attractive than the main narrative. The latter lacks sunshine, etc." Miss Abbott says that she prefers the custom-house sketch to the rest of the book; Coxe and Brownson, much as they disapprove the rest of the book, cannot but approve of the introduction. The earlier reviews are agreed that the story itself is too uniformly gloomy. The *Literary World* implies a preference for the introduction; and *Graham's Magazine* says more explicitly:

In his next work we hope to have a romance equal to the Scarlet Letter in pathos and power, but more relieved by touches of that beautiful and peculiar humor, so serene and searching, in which he excels almost all living writers.

---

[1] Holmes, O. W. *Songs in Many Keys.* Boston 1862. The Study.

In giving voice to this hope Whipple seems to speak for the world. Unadulterated sorrow or unadulterated mirth was not fashionable. The mingling of genres was not only liked by novel readers; it had become a sort of literary fetish. Romantic criticism (especially Coleridge's Shakespearean criticism) had set forth the theory that tragedy and comedy must be combined in any satisfactory work of art—a theory that was peculiarly sympathetic with the sensibilities of the time. Dickens' extraordinary popularity was partly owing to the fact that he was able to supply pathos and humor at the same time, both in the highest degree. *The Scarlet Letter* had provided the two necessary qualities, but in a disjointed fashion; it was natural that the reviewers should demand a combination.

The combination was not long in appearing. *The House of the Seven Gables* was published in April 1851,[1] and it was just the sort of story that Whipple had demanded.

The *Literary World* was again the first magazine to print a notice.[2] The review begins:

In the preface to this work, the anxiously looked for successor to *The Scarlet Letter*, Mr. Hawthorne establishes a separation between the domain of the novel and the romance, and under privilege of the latter, sets up his claim to a certain degree of license in the treatment of the characters and incidents of his coming story. This license, those acquainted with the writer's previous works will readily understand to be in the direction of the spiritualities of the piece, in favor of a process semi-allegorical, by which an acute analysis may be wrought out and truth of feeling be minutely elaborated; an apology in fact, for the preference of character to action, and of character, for that which is allied to the darker elements of life—the dread blossoming of evil in the soul and its fearful retributions. . . .

Verily this Hawthorne retains in him streaks of a Puritan ancestry. Some grave beater of pulpit cushions must be among his ancestry; for of all laymen he will preach to you the closest sermons, probe deepest into the inestimable corruption, carry his lantern, like Belzoni among the mummies, into the most secret recesses of the heart; and he will do this with so vital a force in his propositions that they will transcend the individual example and find a precedent in every reader's heart. So true is it that when once you seize an actual thing you have in it a picture of universal life.

---

[1] *The House of the Seven Gables.* A Romance. By Nathaniel Hawthorne. Boston: Ticknor, Reed and Fields. 1851. 12mo., pp. vi, 344.
[2] *Literary World* (8:334–336) April 26, 1851.

It is obvious from this beginning that Duyckinck can scarcely have heard of the contest over the moral implications of *The Scarlet Letter.* If he had heard of it he could not have assumed so calmly that Hawthorne was something of a Puritan divine. The other reviewers seem to be equally ignorant of any discussion on the moral issue; if they mention the subject at all, it is to praise Hawthorne's purity of tone and meaning.

The rest of the Duyckinck's review is devoted to a long interpretation and explanation of *The House of the Seven Gables.* It is interesting to notice that there is twice as much space devoted to *The House of the Seven Gables* as there had been devoted to *The Scarlet Letter,* and that the tone of the review is different. In the notice of *The Scarlet Letter* the reviewer was concerned with introduction. He explained the character of the work and praised it dogmatically, almost with an air of patronage. In commenting on *The House of the Seven Gables* he scarcely finds it necessary to praise the new book; the merits of the author are now so well known that it is unnecessary to dwell upon them. He gives an elaborate synopsis of the book, adding an appreciative comment here and there. His attempt is to describe the mood of *The House of the Seven Gables* and the impression it leaves upon the reader's mind.

In the *International Monthly Magazine* (a periodical devoted to the less burdensome aspects of art, and, after art, to fashion) appeared in May an article, half review, half essay, called *Nathaniel Hawthorne.*[1] It was written by Rufus W. Griswold, now chiefly and unfavorably remembered as Poe's biographer and literary executor, but then widely known and respected as an editor. He was an indefatigable compiler of collections, two of which, as we have noted, contained some of Hawthorne's writing. The article was headed by an engraved portrait of Hawthorne and began by giving a short account of his life, taken from *Prose Writers in America.* Of *The Scarlet Letter* Griswold says:

> This peculiar and powerful fiction at once arrested attention, and claimed for its author the eminence as a novelist which his previous performances had secured for him as a writer of tales. Its whole atmosphere and the qualities of the characters demanded for a creditable success very unusual capacities. . . .

---

[1] *International Monthly Magazine* (3:156–160) May 1851.

It is a distinction of such works that while they are acceptable to the many, they also surprise and delight the few who appreciate the nicest arrangement and the most high and careful finish. The Scarlet Letter will challenge consideration in the name of Art in the best audience which in any age receives Cervantes, Le Sage, or Scott.

Of *The House of the Seven Gables,* Griswold says: " It is not less original, not less striking, not less powerful, than *The Scarlet Letter."* He concludes with the observation that Hawthorne " is among the first of the first order of our writers, and in their peculiar province, his works are not excelled in the literature of the present day or of the English language."

The *Knickerbocker* of the same month [1] has a routine review on *The House of the Seven Gables.* Clark says very little, except that the book is fascinating, a perfect gallery, and that the author is a man of genius. His last sentence, however, contains a note which may supply some partial reason for the success of Hawthorne's later ventures as against the lack of success that attended his former works. " The volume," says Clark, " is neatly printed, as are all the works which proceed from the flourishing and popular house of the publishers." *The Scarlet Letter* had undoubtedly fared better in a worldly way than its predecessors; it was the first volume of Hawthorne's that issued from a publishing house of prominence and in a form that commanded respect.

There is also a notice in *Harper's Magazine,*[2] which says that while *The House of the Seven Gables* is not as highly wrought as *The Scarlet Letter* it is " more terrific " in conception and not less intense. *The House of the Seven Gables,* in fact, is unsurpassed by anything that Hawthorne has written, for finish, for blending of the tragic and the comic, and for life-like reality.

The *Athenaeum* of May 24th again pronounces judgment on a work of Hawthorne.[3] Chorley writes:

The invention of " The Scarlet Letter " involved so much crime and remorse, that—though never was tragedy on a similar theme more clear of morbid excite-

[1] *Knickerbocker* (37:455–457) May 1851.
[2] *Harper's Magazine* (2:855–856) May 1851.
[3] *Athenaeum* (no. 1230:545–547) May 24, 1851.

ments—we felt that in a journal like ours the tale could be characterized only, not illustrated by extracts. So powerful, however, was the effect of that novel— even on those who, like ourselves, were prepared to receive good things at Mr. Hawthorne's hands—as to justify no ordinary solicitude concerning his next effort in fiction. This is before us in "The House of the Seven Gables": a story widely differing from its predecessor—exceeding it, perhaps, in artistic ingenuity —if less powerful, less painful also—rich in humours and characters—and from first to last individual. It is thus made evident that Mr. Hawthorne possesses the fertility as well as the ambition of Genius; and in sight of these two tales few will dispute his claim to rank among the most original and complete novelists that have appeared in modern times.

Chorley quotes long passages from *The House of the Seven Gables* and praises it highly. He finds in it, however, a dangerous tendency which was not seen in *The Scarlet Letter*—the tendency to play with an idea, to exploit fancy at the expense of the narrative.

The June issue of *Graham's Magazine* contains another review of *The House of the Seven Gables*.[1] It was written by Edwin Percy Whipple. After a few comments on the character of the work, Whipple, returning to the thought in his previous notice, remarks:

> The error in "the Scarlet Letter" proceeded from the divorce of its humor from its pathos—the introduction being as genial as Goldsmith or Lamb, and the story which followed being tragic even to ghastliness. In "the House of Seven Gables" the humor and the pathos are combined.

He finds the same flaw in the work that had been discovered by the reviewer of the *Athenaeum*—that is, a too great infusion of fancy. The fault must be mentioned, he continues, because the book demands, as a right, to be judged by the highest standards of art. Taken as a whole, however, *The House of the Seven Gables* is "Hawthorne's greatest work, and is equally sure of immediate popularity and permanent fame." Whipple concludes:

> "The Scarlet Letter" and "the House of Seven Gables" contain mental qualities which insensibly lead some readers to compare the author to other cherished literary names. Thus we have seen Hawthorne likened for this quality to Goldsmith and for that to Irving, and for still another to Dickens; and some critics have given him the preference over all whom he seems to resemble. But

---

[1] *Graham's Magazine* (38:467–468) June 1851.

the real cause for congratulation in the appearance of an original genius like Hawthorne is not that he dethrones any established prince in literature, but that he founds a new principality of his own.

A short notice of the second edition of *Twice-Told Tales* follows this article.[1]   " The success of *The Scarlet Letter*," says Whipple, " has created an increased demand for the author's other writings." He praises the tales for their fascination of mind, their charm of style, and their novel combination of " mental and moral traits."

It will be seen from these five reviews that the first tendency of the reviewers was to place *The House of the Seven Gables* above *The Scarlet Letter*.   The reason for this we have touched upon before: *The House of the Seven Gables* was exactly the type of story which they had demanded.   It contained laughter and tears, mingled in as nearly even a proportion as well could be.   Humor and pathos were no longer divorced, and the subject of *The House of the Seven Gables,* moreover, was unexceptionable. Objection might be made to a study of adultery, however delicately done; no one could object to a study of avarice.

The House of the Seven Gables undoubtedly set a seal upon Hawthorne's reputation.   Another *Scarlet Letter* could not have established him so plainly.   Not only had he satisfied the demands made of any novelist of the first rank; he had also proved his versatility.   As the *Athenaeum* put it: " It is thus made evident that Mr. Hawthorne possesses the fertility as well as the ambition of Genius."   This last point is important; one of the demands made of a genius in the current romantic criticism was the ability to do a number of things well.   An artist of consequence was supposed to have something of a *weltanschauung;* hypothetically, the more nearly he approached that myriad-minded state of which Shakespeare was the supreme example the higher his rank.

In the meantime, in the *Southern Literary Messenger* for June, we find the first set essay which formally takes Hawthorne's works for its subject.[2]   Its writer, Henry Theodore Tuckerman, who may be

---

[1] Ibid., p. 469.

[2] *Southern Literary Messenger* (17:344–349) June 1851. Republished in Tuckerman, Henry T. *Mental Portraits*, London 1853, pp. 250–270; and in *Littel's Living Age* (81:518–524) June 1, 1864.

regarded as the most eminent American critic of this period, at least in the sense that he devoted himself more seriously and exclusively to criticism than any other writer of reputation, begins with a discussion of the psychological novel as a species. It reveals our own nature, he says, as the miscroscope and the telescope reveal the external universe, disclosing the complex laws that govern our being. Hawthorne's most airy sketches show preoccupation with this process of revelation. His insight is remarkable; his accuracy and his fidelity to detail in local and personal portraiture no less remarkable. His allegories, though they indicate great moral truths, have none of the coldness usually found in allegorical writing. Hawthorne's genius lies in the difficult art of creating a mood; though he never seems to strive for an effect, he gradually succeeds in putting the reader into the proper mental attitude. He touches on all the interests of human life, " now overflowing with a love for external nature, as gentle as that of Thompson, now intent upon the quaint or characteristic in life with a humor as zestful as that of Lamb, now developing the horrible or pathetic with something of Webster's dramatic terror, and again buoyant with a fantasy as aerial as Shelley's conceptions." In every case his invention is adorned with the purest graces of style. The real and the imaginative worlds are marvelously blended in his writings.

But the most elaborate effort of this kind, and the only one, in fact, which seems to have introduced Hawthorne to the whole range of American readers, is " the Scarlet Letter." With all the care in point of style and authenticity which mark his lighter sketches, this genuine and unique romance may be considered as an artistic expression of Puritanism as modified by New England Colonial life. In truth to costume, local manners and scenic features, " the Scarlet Letter " is as reliable as the best of Scott's novels; in the anatomy of human passions and consciousness it resembles the most effective of Balzac's illustrations of Parisian or provincial life, while, in developing bravely and justly the sentiment of the life it depicts, it is as true to humanity as Dickens. . . . Herein is evident and palpable the latent power which we have described as the most remarkable trait of Hawthorne's genius;—the impression grows more significant as we dwell upon the story; the states of mind of the poor Clergyman, Hester, Chillingworth, and Penil [*sic*], being as it were transferred to our bosoms through the intense sympathy their vivid delineation excites;—they seem to conflict, and glow and deepen and blend in our hearts, and finally work out a great moral problem. It is as if we were baptised into the consciousness of Puritan life, of New England character in its elemental state; and knew, by experience, all its frigidity, its gloom, its intellectual enthusiasm and its religious aspiration.

The House of the Seven Gables, Tuckerman concludes, is "a more elaborate and harmonious realization" of the characteristics found in *The Scarlet Letter.*

This enthusiastic essay was followed by another in the *Universalist Quarterly* for July.[1] Its author, Amory Dwight Mayo, who was then at the beginning of his distinguished career as a clergyman, repeats many of Tuckerman's observations. He notices the accuracy of Hawthorne's perception and the beauty of his style. There is a certain tendency to disease in his works, however, which appears in the fearful intensity of his narratives—a tendency which reaches its climax in *The Scarlet Letter.* "In the 'House of Seven Gables,' we see the author struggling out of its grasp with a vigor which we believe insures a final recovery." Hawthorne's peculiar province, proceeds Mayo, is the depiction of the soul's relation to spiritual laws.

We regard him as a religious novelist in a high and peculiar sense. He does not, like the tribe of disguised parsons who have broken into the realm of letters, write books and sew together men and women of pasteboard to illustrate artificial and arbitrary creeds, or rules of conduct. Neither, like the able class which swears by Goethe, does he give a picture of actual life faithful in every particular, leaving the reason to find its law and morality; but he lays bare those spiritual laws of God to which we must conform, and with wonderful distinctness describes the soul's relations to them.

Mayo says of *The Scarlet Letter:*

The story so gracefully introduced, is the most remarkable of Mr. Hawthorne's works, whether we consider felicity of plot, sustained interest of development, analysis of character, or the witchery of a style which invests the whole with a strange ethereal beauty. These qualities of the book are so evident that we now desire to go beneath them to those which make it, in many respects, the most powerful imaginative work of the present era of English literature. No reader possessing the slightest portion of spiritual insight, can fail to perceive that the chief value of the romance is religious. . . .

---

[1] *Universalist Quarterly and General Review* (8:272–293) July 1851.

Standing as "the Scarlet Letter" does, at the junction of several moral highways, it is not easy to grasp the central idea around which it instinctively arranged itself in the author's mind. The most obvious fact upon its pages is, that the only safety for a human soul consists in appearing to be exactly what it is. If holy, it must not wrench itself out of its sphere to become a part in any satanic spectacle; if corrupt, it must heroically stand upon the low ground of its own sinfulness, and rise through penitence and righteousness.

Mayo's opinions are very similar to Loring's it will be seen; the article may be regarded as a reply to Coxe, as Coxe's article had been a reply to Loring.

A notice in the *Southern Quarterly Review* for the same month [1] remarks that Hawthorne is a tale writer rather than a novelist: a peculiarly endowed creator of fresh and delicate prose fancies. His province lies in the subtle region of the heart, and *The House of the Seven Gables* happily exhibits his powers. This novel, the reviewer adds, may prove less attractive than *The Scarlet Letter* because it is less concentrated, but it is more truthful and not less earnest of purpose.

Melville wrote to Hawthorne soon after the publication of *The House of the Seven Gables* including in his letter a review, written as if for publication.[2] He speaks with great appreciation of the rich decoration of the romance and he is particularly struck by the character of Clifford who "is filled with awful truth throughout." "There is a certain tragic phase of humanity," he continues, "which in our opinion was never more powerfully embodied than by Hawthorne. We mean the tragedies of human thought in its own unbiased, native and profounder workings. We think that into no recorded mind has the intense feeling of usable truth ever entered more deeply than into this man's. By usable truth we mean the apprehension of the absolute conditions of present things as they strike the eye of a man who fears them not, though they do their worst to him. . . ." This thought, which is the principal one of the "Virginian" article, sends Melville off in a characteristic burst of feeling. He speaks of God and the universe in large but not very intelligible terms, remarking incidentally that Hawthorne says no! in a voice of

---

[1] *Southern Quarterly Review* (n. s. 4:265–266) July 1851.
[2] See *Nathaniel Hawthorne and his Wife* (1:385–389).

thunder, and that this is the grand truth about him, which distinguishes him forever from the liars who say yes. Then he catches himself up: " What's the reason, Mr. H., that in the last stages of metaphysics a fellow always falls to swearing so? I could rip an hour. You see I begin with a little criticism extracted for your benefit from the ' Pittsfield Secret Review,' and I have landed in Africa."

There is a letter from Lowell [1] in somewhat different style. " I thought I could not forgive you," he wrote, " if you wrote anything better than ' The Scarlet Letter '; but I cannot help believing it a great triumph that you should have been able to deepen and widen the impression made by such a book as that. It seems to me that the ' House ' is the most valuable contribution to New England history that has been made. It is with the highest art that you have typified (in the revived likeness of Judge Pyncheon to his ancestor the Colonel) that intimate relationship between the Present and the Past in the way of ancestry and descent, which historians carefully overlook." Lowell ends his letter by protesting that Hawthorne does not do justice, in his preface to the new edition of *Twice-Told Tales,* to his early reputation. " The augury of a man's popularity," he says, " might be looked for in the intensity and not in the vulgarity of his appreciation."

A dull essay on Hawthorne appeared in the *New Monthly Magazine* for February, 1852. [2] The anonymous writer repeats, more positively, what the reviewer of the *Athenaeum* had said when *The Scarlet Letter* first appeared, referring, like Chorley, to *Adam Blair:* that its subject is dangerous, but treated by Hawthorne with much delicacy, and that the impression left upon the mind of the reader is like that of an excellent sermon. Incidentally the writer of the article confirms the rank that had been given Hawthorne by the American critics by mentioning Irving, and amplifies it by mentioning Cooper. " He is now seated," he says, " upon the same eminence with Cooper and Washington Irving." The American critics never included Cooper among their numerous comparisons, presumably because they were all under the impression that such a comparison could not be flattering. Cooper was, at this period, singularly unhonored in his own country.

---

[1] Ibid. (1:390–392).
[2] *New Monthly Magazine* (94:202–207) February 1852. Reprinted in *Littel's Living Age* (33:11–19) April 3, 1852.

It might be interesting, though not strictly in keeping with our subject, to mention an article on Hawthorne by Paul Emile Dourand Forgues which appeared in the *Revue des Deux Mondes* at this time.[1] It forms part of a series of articles on American writers published during the year by that omniscient journal. Hawthorne and Emerson, Forgues says, have overcome the imputation that American writers derive from English writers. One may say with some reason that Brockden Brown follows Goodwin, Irving Addison, and Cooper Scott, and that there are European prototypes for Bryant and Longfellow; but Hawthorne and Emerson are in their way unique. Hawthorne may be linked with his countryman, Poe, but differs from him in that Poe inhabits an unhealthful and vertiginous region. Poe's effects are striking, but his means are illegitimate and his results eccentric, while Hawthorne has noble instincts and is devoted to truth. Forgues speaks with admiration of *The Scarlet Letter* and mentions its immense success with wonder. He is not prepared to understand by what miracle, in view of the anathemas recently directed against *Lélia* in England, a novel so bold (and more frankly bold than George Sand's) has been able to receive such suffrage and to encounter so little detraction. *The House of the Seven Gables,* he says, is a happy revelation of Hawthorne's talent " dans le choix des couleurs vagues, des harmonies mysterieuses, des formes entrevues, des intuitions étranges qui lui ont permis de raffermir cette trame fatiguée, d'y broder des figures nouvelles, d'y marier aux plus aïgues détails de la vie contemporaine les tientes poètiques du passé."

In *Eliza Cook's Journal* for June,[2] Hawthorne is treated as a philosophical writer of great importance; long passages from the more reflective and dogmatic parts of *The Scarlet Letter* are quoted with comments on their truth and profundity.

The two novels together made a great impression. As Hawthorne wrote to his sister: " I receive very complimentary letters from poets and prosers, and adoring ones from young ladies; and I have almost a challenge from a gentleman who complains of me for introducing his grandfather, Judge Pyncheon." [3]   There was also a stir in Eng-

---

[1] *Revue des Deux Mondes* (14:337–365) April 15, 1852.
[2] *Eliza Cook's Journal* (7:121–124) June 19, 1852.
[3] See Conway's *Life,* pp. 134–135.

land. Mrs. Kemble wrote Hawthorne that the two novels had made
a greater sensation than any book since *Jane Eyre;*[1] and Browning
is reported to have said that Hawthorne was the finest genius that
had appeared in English literature in many years.[2]

The publication of *A Wonder Book for Boys and Girls*[3] and *The
Snow Image and Other Twice-Told Tales,*[4] toward the end of 1851,
occasioned surprisingly little comment. One of the very few notices
received by *The Wonder Book,* that in *The Literary World,*[5] contains, aside from a series of excerpts, only a compliment to the author's
imagination as being " so well under control and in his power that
he may direct its forces either to the terror of age or the amusement
of childhood," and the suggestion that his children's stories are at once
amusing and beneficial—to children. There was little more in the
case of *The Snow Image,* which was a last gathering of tales, most
of them dating from an early period. Hawthorne, with the success
of his first novel, had given up tale writing with relief; and the only
short story which he wrote after the year 1850 is the slight *jeu
d'esprit* " Feathertop " which was published in a magazine and later
included in the second edition of *Mosses.* The *Southern Quarterly
Review,*[6] and *Today*[7] have a mere word or two of commendation
for *The Snow Image; The Literary World*[8] and *Graham's*[9] have
notices only slightly more elaborate. The *Literary World* (that is
to say the faithful Duyckinck) gives extended quotations with appreciative comments under the general heading " Another choice gathering golden thoughts from the old placer." *Graham's* says of the
first tale in the volume that it is " one of those delicate creations which
no imagination less aetherial and shaping than Hawthorne's could
body forth." The reviewer adds that to the thoughtful reader the

---

[1] See Fields' *Hawthorne,* p. 34.

[2] See *Memories of Hawthorne,* p. 174.

[3] *A Wonder Book for Boys and Girls.* By Nathaniel Hawthorne, with Engravings by Baker from Designs by Billings. Boston: Ticknor, Reed and Fields.
1852. 16mo., pp. vi. 256.

[4] *The Snow Image and Other Twice-Told Tales.* By Nathaniel Hawthorne.
Boston: Ticknor, Reed & Fields. 12mo., pp. 273.

[5] *Literary World* (9:424-425) November 29, 1851.

[6] *Southern Quarterly Review* (n. s. 5:262) January 1852.

[7] *Today* (1:8) January 3, 1852.

[8] *Literary World* (10:22-27) January 10, 1852.

[9] *Graham's Magazine* (40:433) April 1852.

tales are not merely arresting; they are " contributions to the philosophy of the human mind." They can hardly add to Hawthorne's great
reputation, he says, but they fully sustain it.

The publication of *The Blithedale Romance* in May, 1852, caused
another series of reviews.[1] The first notices that we find are English.

The *New Monthly Magazine* [2] contains a detailed synopsis of the
story and a number of excerpts accompanied by admiring comments,
with a note about Hawthorne's great reputation on both sides of the
Atlantic. The *Spectator* [3] contains a review which begins by placing Hawthorne as " an American writer of considerable repute in his
own country, and of high though limited appreciation here." His
novels, the *Spectator* continues, are of a peculiar kind, their interest
not depending upon incident like most novels of the romantic school
but upon detail. " This manner might probably run into tediousness,
and the singularity verge upon plagiarism, were the thesis European
and hackneyed. But Mr. Hawthorne, by taking his subjects from the
actual life or traditions of America, gives to his detailed pictures an
attraction of novelty to English readers, while the just delineation
and easy elegance of his pen impart an air of vivid truthfulness to his
reflections and elaborate descriptions." The *Spectator* criticizes adversely the imperfect plot of *The Blithedale Romance;* and then goes
on at some length in praise of the two important morals conveyed,
the first dealing with the danger of a woman's deviating from accepted usage, and the second and more important dealing with the
dangers of philanthropy. This second moral cannot be too strongly
impressed, in the opinion of the *Spectator;* for unwise philanthropy
" actuates classes as well as individuals, and with a less sense of responsibility " and has been responsible for the ruin of the British West
Indies and for the aggravated miseries of the African race.

Henry Chorley says in the *Athenaeum* a few days later [4] that, while
some of Hawthorne's readers may be disappointed in finding that he

[1] *The Blithedale Romance.* By Nathaniel Hawthorne. Boston: Ticknor, Reed
and Fields. 1852. 12mo., pp. viii, 288.
[2] *New Monthly Magazine* (95:334–343) July 1852. Reprinted in *Littel's Living Age* (34:327–332) August 14, 1852.
[3] *Spectator* (25:637–638) July 3, 1852. Partially reprinted in *Littel's Living
Age* (34:332) August 14, 1852.
[4] *Athenaeum* (pp. 741–743) July 10, 1852.

has produced a story of a new kind, as some of Scott's readers were disappointed with *The Antiquary,* nevertheless *The Blithedale Romance* " puts the seal on the reputation of its author as the highest, deepest and finest imaginative writer whom America has yet produced." Chorley felicitates himself upon the fulfillment of his early confidence in Hawthorne's talent; and he praises the book in unreserved terms, for the profundity of its moral, for its fine description of character, and (oddly enough) for the perfection of its plot.

The first American notice appeared in *Today* on the seventeenth of July.[1] It was probably written by the editor, Charles Hale, and it shows a good deal of suppressed indignation against Hawthorne for his disrespectful treatment of some ideas dear to the hearts of Boston liberals. *The Blithedale Romance,* says the reviewer, is marked by all the beauties and all the faults of Hawthorne's genius. It is full of graceful description, dancing humor, delicate appreciation of character, and so on; it is marred by a confused and confusing plot with a melodramatic ending; and it presents an imperfect picture of society. " We can hardly avoid the feeling that a covert sneer at that which is considered good by those who live ' in the world,' and also at those who would try to live above the things of the world, imbues every chapter." The reviewer says, in conclusion and in extenuation, that he would not have dwelt upon the faults of the novel, if its merits were not easily recognized by every intelligent reader.

The *Literary World* printed an unusual notice some days later [2] (the notice of June 5th merely reprinted the preface of *The Blithedale Romance* and gave a few notes on Brook Farm) which is undoubtedly not by Duychinck. The reviewer wishes that Hawthorne had treated the " æsthetic labor establishment at Roxbury " in a more matter-of-fact way. Good-humored laughter would have been more appropriate to the subject than Hawthorne's spiritual anatomy, he says; and he goes on to object to " spiritualities " in general. " It may be a searching conscientious operation on rare occasions to take our spirits out of their bodily cases and look at them nakedly, even in the thin, dry atmosphere of New England speculation; but we are convinced that, for the ordinary entertainment of life, such spectacles

---

[1] *Today* (2: 42) July 17, 1852.
[2] *Literary World* (11:52–54) July 24, 1852.

are, to say the least, unprofitable." The reviewer however ends by quoting with great appreciation the passages in which Hawthorne comments maliciously on Fourierism and reform, and by saying:

> The spiritualities and more powerful scenes of this book are not to be brought into the glare of a weekly newspaper. The reader will find them in the volume, of a strength and nicety of grasp not inferior to the hand-writing of the *Scarlet Letter,* or the tragedy of the *Seven Gables.*

Whipple's review in the September issue of *Graham's Magazine* is elaborate.[1] It begins with a word about Hawthorne's originality, and a comment on his style, which " reminds us of the style of Addison, of Scott and of Irving " though it is as original as his substance. His works are " an entirely new product of the human mind." Of the *Scarlet Letter* it says:

> In " The Scarlet Letter," which made a deeper impression upon the public than any romance ever published in the United States, there is little true characterization, in the ordinary meaning of the term. . . . It is the law and not the person that is vitally conceived, and accordingly the author traces its sure operation with an unshrinking intellect that, for the time, is remorseless to persons. As an illustration of the divine order on which our conventional order rests, it is the most moral book of the age; and is especially valuable as demonstrating the superficiality of that code of ethics, predominant in the French school of romance, which teaches obedience to individual instinct and impulse, regardless of moral truths which contain the generalized experience of the race. The purpose of the book did not admit of geniality. Adultery has been made genial by many poets and novelists, but only by considering it under a totally different aspect from that in which Hawthorne viewed it. Geniality in " The Scarlet Letter " would be like an ice-cream shop in Dante's Inferno.

Returning to the original subject, Whipple says of the new work:

> " The Blithedale Romance," just published, seems to us the most perfect in the execution of any of Hawthorne's works, and as a work of art, hardly equalled by anything else which the country has produced. It is a real organism of the mind, with the strict unity of one of Nature's own creations.

William Pike, Hawthorne's former associate in the Salem custom-house and his highly respected friend, gave an opinion of *The Blithe-*

---

[1] *Graham's Magazine* (41: 333–334) September 1852.

dale Romance by letter in response to Hawthorne's anxious request.[1] Pike was a self-educated Swedenborgian, one among those many profound thinkers in every walk of life and of every shade of opinion who gave such a peculiar and interesting aspect to the New England of that era. He says that *The Blithedale Romance* probes deeply. "Almost all the novel writers I have read, though truthful to nature, go through only some of the strata; but you are the only one who breaks through the hard-pan—who accounts for that class of actions and manifestations in men so inexplicable as to call forth the exclamation, ' How strangely that man acts! what a fool he is!' and the like!" He praises the novel's exposition of the passion of love, and goes on to explain his own ideas upon love, which are remarkable but not very relevant to the motives in *The Blithedale Romance.* He concludes: "I think Blithedale more profound in maxims than any work of years. They will be quoted in the future as texts. You hit off the follies and errors of man with a quick humor, as no other man does. . . . You make us think the more and resolve the better, because the smart is not so sharp that we have to stop thinking to rub the wound."

Hillard refused to draw comparisons between *The Blithedale Romance* and Hawthorne's other romances.[2] He thinks Zenobia a splendid creature, though he wishes that Hawthorne had not killed her or at least that he had given her a drier and handsomer death; and he says that Priscilla is "an exquisite nature." There were others, however, who were relatively more appreciative of *The Blithedale Romance.* Browning, when Hawthorne met him in England in 1856, said that it was his favorite.[3] He did not offer any explanation of his preference; but the explanation lies no doubt in the principal motive of the book and in the characters of the two protagonists, which fell in with his taste for high-wrought mental conflicts and for "passionate" characters. Ellery Channing agreed with Browning's preference.[4] He says, somewhat enigmatically, that no book was ever printed "containing better effects for illustration." Howells [5] was

---

[1] See *Nathaniel Hawthorne and his Wife* (1: 444–447).
[2] Ibid. (1: 448).
[3] See *Notes of Travel* (2:185).
[4] See *Nathaniel Hawthorne and his Wife* (2:264–265).
[5] Howells, W. D. *My Literary Passions.*

later to say that he liked *The Blithedale Romance* best because it seemed to him more realistic than the others, though certainly upon this point Henry James must be the sounder critic, who heard more of the "vague hum" of life in *The House of the Seven Gables*.

In spite of the fact that Whipple (who could scarcely in friendship suggest failing powers) declares that *The Blithedale Romance* is the best of Hawthorne's works, in spite of the fact that the reviews are in general commendatory, *The Blithedale Romance* was rather coolly received in America. If anything, it seems to have diminished Hawthorne's reputation as an artist. The book is, in fact, almost a parody of Hawthorne's usual manner. Similar but weaker motives are substituted in *The Blithedale Romance* for those which had appeared in *The Scarlet Letter* and *The House of Seven Gables:* mesmerism takes the place of witchcraft, the artificial world of Brook Farm takes the place of the highly concentrated world of New England Puritanism, Zenobia takes the place of Hester. Readers, whether consciously or not, must in general have felt this diluted quality; and their natural tendency was to revise their estimation of Hawthorne's other works in the light of *The Blithedale Romance*. The new book cast an air of disillusion over the old.

In the meanwhile Hawthorne had yielded to the request of his old college companion Franklin Pierce and had consented to write a campaign biography. The *Life of Franklin Pierce* [1] was published early in September, or just about the time that the world was beginning to read *The Blithedale Romance;* and it caused a considerable stir. The Whig newspapers, always anxious to find an issue, condemned Hawthorne for prostituting his talents in the current vigorous terms. Although there was no reason why he should not support his party and his friend in this manner, and although the biography was perfectly fair and truthful (the Democratic Review, [2] indeed, revealed a little disappointment under its pride in pointing out that there was no flattery) many of Hawthorne's friends and supporters felt that he should not have actively aided a politician who was allied with the slavery interests. The contest even reached the magazines. Duyckinck

---

[1] *Life of Franklin Pierce.* By Nathaniel Hawthorne. Boston, Ticknor, Reed and Fields. 1852. 12mo., pp. 44.

[2] *Democratic Review* (31: 276–288) September 1852. Hawthorne's Life of Pierce. Perspective.

at any rate undertook to defend Hawthorne in the *Literary World*.[1] He deprecates Hawthorne's deprecatory preface, and says that men of letters not only should be permitted, but even should be encouraged to enter politics. As for the assumption that the biography was written in the hope of obtaining an office, he states his opinion (one of long standing, as we have seen) that the state as a matter of course should enable poets to live. He furthermore thinks that his entry into politics has been of great personal advantage to Hawthorne. " It has brought him down from the subtle metaphysical analysis," he says, " in which his pen has had somewhat too limited and painful a range, to a healthy encounter with living interests. There is no obscure subtlety or attenuated moonshine to be endured in the life of a democratic candidate for the Presidency."

In spite of Duyckinck's sensible defense, the two works published almost simultaneously could not but associate themselves significantly in the minds of readers. The *Life of Pierce* seemed to throw light upon the principles of *The Blithedale Romance* and to emphasize, or to intrude, a note of absolute cynicism into the novel. In any case we have a series of disparaging comments on Hawthorne. The attacks are not direct and pointed as Brownson's and Coxe's had been ; they have no particular object in view and they concern themselves, avowedly at least, with aims that are rather artistic than religious or political. The moral issue, which one might have thought safely buried under the mass of commendation which we have quoted above, is again revived. The chief point of offense in *The Blithedale Romance,* apparently, was the character of Zenobia and the warmth of coloring with which it was drawn. The question once raised, Hawthorne's other works suffered equally with *The Blithedale Romance,* by reconsideration of their moral aim.

Today, in its issue of September 18th,[2] published another unfavorable comment by the same writer. Mr. Hawthorne's name, Hale begins, is doubtless destined to immortality, but nevertheless his work contains the gravest flaws. First, he never varies the tone of his conversation; all his characters " talk in the same strain of measured

---

[1] *Literary World* (11: 195–196) September 25, 1852. Hawthorne's Life of Pierce.

[2] *Today* (2:177–181) September 18, 1852.

eloquence." Second, he has no moral teaching; his works seem to imply that life is hollow and meaningless. Third, he has " a tendency toward voluptuousness, possibly coarseness, indicated by the over-coloring of his pictures of physical beauty, and in other ways that we need not particularize." Fourth, his women are peculiar: they illustrate the fact that he has not a broad and entire view of human nature. Of *The Scarlet Letter* Hale says:

> When the " Scarlet Letter " was announced, we expected, judging from the character of his former works, some quaint delineation of Puritan life and character. But the story is an awful probing into the most forbidden regions of human consciousness. It is gloomy from beginning to end. The plot serves only to develop the deep and unnatural plot of Chillingworth, so refined and subtle as to make this part of the book a metaphysical curiosity. . . .

And so on. The article, like Brownson's, points out the fact that the sin in *The Scarlet Letter* was not repented and that the whole philosophy of the three novels, if not actually wrong, is demoralizing. Mingled with these points of blame, the reviewer however includes the usual compliments upon Hawthorne's style. He concludes with an ironical defense of Hawthorne's dereliction to politics, remarking that it is no doubt very easy to appreciate the virtues of a friend who is running for the presidency and who will have a snug little office to bestow.

Brownson, characteristically enough, has almost changed his mind about Hawthorne; his comment on *The Blithedale Romance* is nearly favorable.[1] He complacently refers to his article of 1842 in which he had said that Hawthorne was fitted to stand at the head of American literature; and remarks that, while the assertion seemed extravagant at the time, it has been justified. He wishes for more healthiness of spirit, and he comments adversely (and quite justly) upon some of the character drawing; but he likes the able exposé of Fourierism and philanthropy. The novel is a very able satire on socialistic ideas, he says, and " in this point of view, we can commend *The Blithedale Romance,* not as unobjectionable, indeed, but as little so as we can expect any popular work to be that emanates from an uncatholic source."

---

[1] *Brownson's Quarterly Review* (n. s. 6: 561–564) October 1852.

The *American Whig Review*, glad to seize an opportunity to attack the author of the *Life of Franklin Pierce*, takes up the current discussion of Hawthorne's art and morals.[1] There is a veil of unreality over *The Blithedale Romance*, says the reviewer, which is owing to the sluggish antiquity of its style—a style perhaps suited to *The Scarlet Letter*, but not to a tale of the present day.

> Mr. Hawthorne deals artistically with shadows. There is a strange, unearthly fascination about the fair spectres that throng his works, and we know no man who can distort nature, or idealize abortions more cleverly than the author of the Scarlet Letter. But we question much, if we strip Mr. Hawthorne's works of a certain beauty and originality which they are always sure to possess, whether the path he has chosen is a healthy one. . . . It is not alone necessary to produce works of art. The soul of beauty is Truth and Truth is ever progressive. . . . His men are either vicious, crazed or misanthropical, and his women are either unwomanly, unearthly or unhappy.

Apropos the *Life of Franklin Pierce*, the reviewer remarks in conclusion:

> Give us works as the *Scarlet Letter* and the *Blithedale Romance*—works of art and beauty, with all their deformities—and let your rare genius soar forever above the atmosphere of mushroom heroes and penny biographies.

In October a notice appeared in the *New Quarterly Review*[2] (London) of a highly unfavorable kind, though not influenced by political considerations. The story is retold in semi-burlesque style to show the oddity of the characters in it; and morbidity and exaggeration are said to be characteristic of the author. " He is in his element when dissecting a corpse and smelling putrefaction." The hesitation and the lack of coherence and plan in the novel are ascribed to Hawthorne's want of moral earnestness. The ironical pictures of socialistic life are however much relished; and, perhaps for this reason, *The Blithedale Romance* is declared the best of Hawthorne's productions.

Another English periodical, the *Westminster Review*, has a better article.[3] It begins with a reference to the popularity of *Uncle Tom's*

---

[1] *American Whig Review* (16: 417–424) November 1852.

[2] *New Quarterly Review* (1:413–415) October 1852.

[3] *Westminster Review* (58:592–598) October 1852.

Cabin, remarking that *The Blithedale Romance* is in no danger of such attention though " it is unmistakably the finest production of genius in either hemisphere, for this quarter at least." The reviewer then proceeds to take exception to the book. The characters are so minutely analyzed and so completely individualized that there can be no dramatic cooperation, nor any of that graduated subordination to each other which gives harmony and unity to a narrative and concentrated force to its issue. They are not drawn into relationship; they are simply contemporaries remarkable for their points of mutual repulsion. The reviewer objects especially to Zenobia's fate, on the ground that it is unreasonable in view of her character. He points out that there are too many moral applications. " So many morals— one apiece for Coverdale and Hollingsworth, and two and a half for Zenobia—are symptomatic of weak moral purpose." He protests against the unrealistic treatment of highly interesting material and remarks that the socialistic element, if decorative, is at variance with purposes of the narrative. " Zenobia's life would have been exhibited with more propriety," he says, " and its moral brought home with more effect in the ' theatre ' of the world, out of which it really grew and of which it would have formed a vital and harmonious part." The reviewer mingles these unimpeachable strictures with a few commonplace comments upon the " poetry of the dissecting room " ; but his article, formless and sometimes self-contradictory as it is, reveals a more stable point of view than we have found elsewhere, and something like a grasp upon a new set of critical principles. It is " realistic " criticism in its germ, although the term *realism* as representing a school of thought had not yet been invented; and it reveals that the work of the great English novelists of this period, the work of Thackeray and George Eliot let us say, had begun to make a solid, if involuntary, impression upon critical judgment in England.

In the same month the *Southern Quarterly Review*[1] has a notice which deals with the burning problem of Zenobia in a simpler fashion. " Instead of Zenobia committing suicide, an action equally shocking and unnecessary," says the reviewer, " he [Hawthorne] should have converted her, by marriage—the best remedy for such a case—from

---

[1] *Southern Quarterly Review* (n. s. 16: 543) October 1853.

the error of her ways, and left her, a mother, with good prospects of a numerous progeny."

During the course of the year Miss Mitford published her *Recollections of a Literary Life*,[1] which is surely the most artless book of literary criticism ever writen. She writes about dozens of writers, living and dead, quite as if they were all her friends and neighbors; and she includes a number of American writers among them. She regarded herself, indeed, as the special friend and advocate of America; and certainly she could boast of a wider acquaintance with American writing than could most English critics. In the chapter on Hawthorne she tells the stories of *The Scarlet Letter* and *The House of the Seven Gables,* seeing no harm in either, though impressed by their " intensity." She speaks of his power of supernatural suggestion (as she does of every other quality) with enthusiasm. " The mixture of the grotesque and the supernatural in Hoffman and the German School, seems coarse and vulgar in comparison." She regards him as the new glory of American literature; and she is much impressed by his portrait—" what a head! and he is said to be of the height and build of Daniel Webster. So much the better. It is well that a fine intellect should be fitly lodged; harmony is among the rarest."

Toward the end of the year George William Curtis published his *Homes of American Authors*,[2] including a chapter upon Hawthorne's old residence in a collection which deals only with the most eminent American men of letters, with Emerson, Bryant, Prescott, Lowell, Audubon, Irving, Everett, Longfellow and Bancroft,—that is to say, with the evident immortals. The chapter consists largely of a romanticized account of Hawthorne's secluded life in Concord (he was " phantom and a fable " to the villagers, says Curtis) and with a description of his character, exaggerating its poetic remoteness. *The Scarlet Letter,* he says, placed Hawthorne among " the world's masters of romance "; and *The House of the Seven Gables* more deeply confirmed that position. " It is the same black canvas upon which plays the rainbow-flash of his fancy, never, in its brightest

---

[1] Mitford, Mary Russell. *Recollections of a Literary Life.* New York 1852 (pp. 525–531).
[2] Curtis, George William. *Homes of American Authors.* New York 1853 (pp. 289–313). (It was published in 1852.)

moment, more illuminating than the gloom. This marks all his writings. They have a terrible beauty, like the Siren, and their fascination is sure."

In the *North American Review* for January 1853, an unfavorable criticism again appears.[1] Andrew Preston Peabody in reviewing *The House of the Seven Gables* and *The Blithedale Romance* repeats a great many of Coxe's observations. The chief basis of his former enthusiasm having been destroyed, Peabody has revised his judgment. Hawthorne has original powers, he observes, and his works are impressive; nevertheless he has written " nothing more likely to survive his times than several simply, yet gorgeously, wrought and highly suggestive allegories, among which ' The Celestial Railroad ' holds the first place, and deserves an immortality coeval with that of the great prose-epic which furnished its theme." Hawthorne's history is untrustworthy in spirit, if accurate in detail.

> Thus in the " Scarlet Letter," he has at once depicted the exterior of early New England life with a fidelity that might shame the most accurate chronicler, and defaced it by passions too fierce and wild to have been stimulated to their desolating energy under colder skies than those of Spain and Italy. At the same time, he has unwittingly defamed the fathers of New England, by locating his pictures of gross impurity and sacrilegious vice where no shadow of reproach, and no breath but of immaculate fame, had ever rested before. He thus has violated one of the most sacred canons of literary creation.

Peabody remarks that *The House of the Seven Gables* has been most successful with the public and deserves to be; but that *The Blithedale Romance,* inferior as it is, has the merit of exposing socialism and its threat against the stability of the family.

Hawthorne found a biographer in Richard Henry Stoddard, who had recently scraped an acquaintance with him. The article was published in the *National Magazine* for January 1853.[2] Its sketch of Hawthorne's life is interesting because it was largely quoted (with substitution of the third person for the first) from an autobiographical letter. Hawthorne's temperament, says Stoddard, is vividly reflected in his works. The seclusion and dreaming of his life is mirrored in

---

[1] *North American Review* (76:227–248) January 1853.
[2] *National Magazine* (2:17–24) January 1853.

the novels and the tales. Here, like Curtis, Stoddard gives a romantic description of Hawthorne's seclusion. The virtues of his writing are those of poetry rather than those of prose, he says. He praises the " simplicity, purity and beauty " of Hawthorne's style as being better than Irving's and better than Addison's. He quotes Poe on the perfection of his technique. Hawthorne is a severe moralist, he adds in conclusion, and this moral uprightness is his chief merit, in an age when many beautiful works have an evil and unhealthy tendency.

During the course of 1853 there were few other American comments on Hawthorne. The publication of *Tanglewood Tales* [1] in August occasioned no more critical interest than the publication of his previous children's stories. Whipple dropped a flattering word about them in the *Literary World;* [2] there was a short notice in *Graham's* [3] mistakenly headed " Inglewood Tales " in which the reviewer remarks that the tales are pure and wholesome, showing no trace of that morbid analysis " which lends a fascination, sometimes serpentlike, to Hawthorne's novels." However Tuckerman in his " A Sketch of American Literature " [4] treats Hawthorne at respectful length, repeating the ideas found in his earlier article in the *Southern Literary Messenger,* but with increased emphasis and authority as being now supported by public verdict. And Whipple in his essay called " The Ludicrous Side of Life " [5] pays his friend a magnificent tribute. After running through a long list of such eminent practitioners of the humorous as Goethe, Ben Jonson, Sheridan, Irving, Pope and Addison, he remarks that Hawthorne " whose beautiful depth of cheerful feeling is the very poetry of mirth " deserves a place second to none. He adds: " In ease, grace, delicate sharpness of satire—in a felicity of touch which often surpasses the felicity of Addison, in a subtlety of insight which often reaches further than the subtlety of Steele—the humor of Hawthorne presents traits so fine as to be almost too excellent for popularity, as, to everyone who has

[1] *Tanglewood Tales;* Being a Second Wonder Book, with Fine Illustrations. By Nathaniel Hawthorne. Boston: Ticknor, Reed and Fields. 1853.
[2] *Literary World* (13:99–101) September 10, 1853.
[3] *Graham's Magazine* (43:333–335) September 1853.
[4] Tuckerman, Henry T. *A Sketch of American Literature.* In Shaw, Thomas B. *Outlines of English Literature.* Philadelphia 1853 (pp. 465–466).
[5] Whipple, Edwin Percy. *Lectures on Subjects Connected with Literature and Life.* Boston 1863. The Ludicrious Side of Life, pp. 122–155.

attempted their criticism, they are too refined for statement. The brilliant atoms flit, hover and glance before our minds, but the remote sources of their ethereal light lie beyond our analysis,—

> ' And no speed of ours avails
> To hunt upon their shining trails.' "

There were two interesting British articles during the year, one in the *New Monthly Magazine* for June,[1] and the other in the *North British Review* for November.[2]   The articles are a reminder that Hawthorne's works had sold rather better in England than in America; in 1851 there had been five London editions of *Twice-Told Tales,* three of *The Scarlet Letter,* and two of the *House of Seven Gables.* Most of these were cheap editions, *Railway Series* or *Shilling Libraries.* Strangely enough, both of these articles prefer *The Blithedale Romance* to Hawthorne's other writings. The *New Monthly Magazine* article, which was written by the same reviewer who had earlier commented upon Hawthorne, says: " *The Blithedale Romance* we esteem, in spite of its coming last, the highest and best of Mr. Hawthorne's works. The tale is narrated with more ingenuity and ease; the characters are at least equal to their predecessors, and the style is at once richer and more robust—more mellowed, and yet more pointed and distinct." The reviewer pays a high compliment to *A Wonder Book,* in this respect differing from the American critics, who are all inclined to pass over the children's books in silence.

The article from the *North British Review* is called " American Novels " ; it comments briefly on two of Longfellow's novels, on two of Elizabeth Wetherell's, and on *Uncle Tom's Cabin,* but it is chiefly concerned with Hawthorne. Hawthorne's novels, the essayist states, are " the most forcible in the imaginative line that America has yet produced." Hawthorne's tendency to fatalism is not approved, though *The Scarlet Letter* is a wonderful *tour de force* in the analysis of character. " We know nothing equal to it, in its way, in the whole court of English literature." The reviewer concludes: " Mr. Haw-

---

[1] *New Monthly Magazine* (98: 202–212) June 1853. Reprinted in *Littel's Living Age* (38: 154–160) July 16, 1853.
[2] *North British Review* (20: 81–99) November 1853. Reprinted in *Littel's Living Age* (40: 51–59) January 7, 1854.

thorne's chef d'oeuvre is, however, his last work, 'The Blithedale Romance '; it is the best novel in America, and one of the best of the present age."

This British preference for *The Blithedale Romance* is inexplicable unless, perhaps, by the fact that Hawthorne's other works were so much read and so commonly, not to say vulgarly, known that a reviewer who valued his originality could not but recommend the work which was still comparatively unfamiliar. Perhaps the sound conservative ideas expressed in the novel had a tendency to promote artistic appreciation. The *North British Review,* indeed, quotes all of Hawthorne's dicta upon feminism and philanthropy.

In 1854 Hawthorne found another biographer, George Washington Bungay, who included him along with some eighty other more or less eminent persons in *Off-Hand Takings*.[1] Bungay has evidently heard the story of Hawthorne's elusiveness. More importantly, *The Scarlet Letter* was included among Henry Giles' *Illustrations of Genius*,[2] as a notable contribution to the inspired creations of the human mind. Giles was an Irish-born Unitarian who had become a very popular lecturer in the United States. *The Scarlet Letter,* he says, has all the peculiarities of its author's genius but "of his genius put forth with a strength beyond any former effort." He gives an excellent analysis of the book with emphasis on its moral teaching, and he displays an enthusiasm which we have met elsewhere for little Pearl. She is more appealing in her delicate witchery, he says, than the Mignon of Goethe, the Fenella of Scott or the Little Nell of Dickens. The story has no formal moral, he adds, but it contains admirable lessons in character and in the relations between society and the individual.

So far as periodicals go, we have in this year only an essay in the *Yale Literary Magazine*.[3] It is written in the best prize-essay style, and its writer was more concerned with the aims of art in general than with the particular artist whose name stood at the head of his

---

[1] Bungay, George Washington. *Off-Hand Takings; or Crayon Sketches of the Noticeable Men of our Age.* New York 1854. Nathaniel Hawthorne (pp. 210–213).
[2] Giles, Henry. *Illustrations of Genius.* Boston 1854. The Scarlet Letter (pp. 66–90).
[3] *Yale Literary Magazine* (19:252–255) June 1854.

paper. What little is said of Hawthorne is commendatory; he is praised for the usual qualities—imagination, power of analysis, beauty of style.

British interest in Hawthorne continued actively and we find in the course of 1855 three painstaking articles. *Tait's Edinburgh Magazine* [1] published an odd and interesting essay upon American literature which deals largely with Hawthorne's work. It begins with a protest against the superciliousness of English critics and against their assumption that American writers are uninitiative. American literature, says the writer, is necessarily a continuation of English literature; and one should hope to see them draw closer together rather than diverge from each other. And in any case, he continues, American authors have just now a great influence with us; it should be remembered that, next to Dickens, Longfellow has most powerfully assisted in moulding middle class thought and feeling in this country. He proceeds to compare Hawthorne and Poe. Poe, he says, is a consummate artist but he lacks the element of conscience and feeling; Hawthorne may be his inferior in analytical talent and constructive tact, but he is infinitely his superior in insight and ideality. " Hawthorne does not rank so high among men of genius, as Poe among men of talent—but a man of *genius* he is, if words mean any-thing." Hawthorne resembles Emerson in some ways, he says, and it is his opinion that if Emerson had decided to write a short story he would have written " The Artist of the Beautiful." *The Scarlet Letter* and *The House of the Seven Gables* are deservedly his most popular works, although *The Scarlet Letter* is rather painful and its moral does not satisfy the moral sense. Nevertheless, the treatment of the subject is unexceptionable; Hawthorne is " the most pure minded of story tellers, absolutely *the* most free from grossness." The writer cites several examples of Hawthorne's delicacy. There is a typical meaning running through all of Hawthorne's stories, he continues, and then he goes on to explain *The House of the Seven Gables* as a social allegory—the first example of this kind of Haw-thorne interpretation. Judge Pyncheon, he says, is Might; the Maule family is dispossessed Labor and Industry; Hepzibah represents Aristocracy, Uncle Zenner Poverty, and Phoebe the Middle Classes.

---

[1] *Tait's Edinburgh Magazine* (22: 33–41) January 1855.

He concludes by repeating his contrast between Poe and Hawthorne. We find an article called " Modern Novelists Great and Small " in the May issue of *Blackwood's Magazine*.[1] It deals largely with Hawthorne's work. *Blackwood's,* in its usual downright style, declares that "the anatomy of character" as done in America is not pleasant nor praiseworthy. The essayist is not sure whether he is justified in placing the name of an American " in the foremost rank of our secondary eminences." Had the reputation of Hawthorne been confined to America, it would have been out of the sphere of comment; but his novels have created as much excitement in England as those of Miss Brontë. His work is too feverish; in *The Scarlet Letter* " it is not the glow of natural life, but the hectic of disease which burns upon the cheeks of the actors." Hawthorne's fatalism is depressing. In fact, Hawthorne is one of those writers who mistakenly address themselves to an exclusive audience; the true audience of a novelist is the common people.

An article in the *Dublin University Magazine* for October[2] begins by humorously deprecating the recent critique (*Blackwood's* is understood) which complains of Hawthorne's deleterious influence. The influence need not be much feared, for it is confined to a small circle of enthusiasts. Hawthorne, the writer continues, is a perfectly original writer, although he sometimes suggests the quaint still humor of Lamb, the delicate imperceptible touches of Longfellow, or the calm genial flow of Helps. He praises the simplicity of Hawthorne's style, and the manner in which it seems sometimes to express the reader's unexpressed or inexpressible thoughts. Hawthorne does, however, sometimes overreach himself; some of the tales in *Twice-Told Tales* and even in *Mosses from an Old Manse* are flat and uninteresting. *The House of the Seven Gables* in the opinion of the writer is " the most complete and pleasing of Hawthorne's tales," though he complains that Hawthorne emulates the Ancient Mariner in compelling the reader's fascinated attention—and has no story to tell in the end. *The Scarlet Letter,* though the most popular of his works, is feverish and open to the charge of encouraging morbidity.

---

[1] *Blackwood's Magazine* (77: 562–566) May 1855. Reprinted in *Littel's Living Age* (45: 649–652) June 16, 1855.

[2] *Dublin University Magazine* (46:463–469) October 1855. Reprinted in *Eclectic Magazine* (36: 996–1001) November 1855.

The Blithedale Romance is open to ridicule, especially in respect to its characters, but like the rest of Hawthorne's romances, is full of charming description. The *Life of Pierce* is unworthy of its author. The writer concludes his comments on Hawthorne by quoting the assertion of "one of his American critics" (Whipple in "The Ludicrous Side of Life"), that Hawthorne presents traits so fine as to be almost too excellent for popularity.

In the *Harvard Magazine* for July of the same year [1] we find a renewal of the quarrel against Hawthorne. Charles Francis Adams, not then as well known as he was destined to become, begins his essay:

> Among American writers of fiction, with us at least, Hawthorne stands forth pre-eminent. We do not consider it a very agreeable pre-eminence, nor do we envy him his fame. His talents are rather remarkable than attractive, and his exaltation in our eyes partakes somewhat of the nature of gibbeting.

Adams disposes of the other American writers of fiction (Cooper, Brown, Irving, Longfellow, Mrs. Stowe and Mrs. Warner) with a few unenthusiastic words. It is Hawthorne, he says, who has discovered the proper field of American fiction. His characters, nevertheless, are unnatural, and his habit of mind is fleshly. The claim is sometimes made that Hawthorne's books are positively immoral; "for instance, all the troubles and trials, and mortifications of seven years have no effect in 'chastening' Hester Prynne; no pointed moral is drawn to terrify all future deservers of the same dreadful burden of the Scarlet Letter." However:

> That there is any direct and forcible moral conveyed by Hawthorne, it is not our intention to assert, nor do we think his writings injured by its absence, but on the other hand, we can see nothing immoral in them, or conveying a pernicious principle.

Adams concludes his essay by pointing out that Hester's devotion to Dimmesdale is better than the so-called virtue of women who marry for convenience.

One may see, from this essay, that the railing we heard in 1852 is dying out in babble. Undergraduate opinion, whatever claims to originality and independence it may make, is often a rather accurate index of current opinion; and the undergraduate essayist in this case obviously does not know what to think. He is not sure whether *The*

---

[1] *Harvard Magazine* (1: 330–335) July 1855. Hawthorne.

Scarlet Letter is a moral book or not; he begins by being caustic about it and ends by defending it. The sentence which we have quoted, beginning " That there is any direct and forcible moral ———," is admirably expressive because it is so admirably meaningless. Opinion, in other words, was beginning to waver, and in any case the problem scarcely seemed as important as once it had.

Hawthorne, in fact, no longer commanded the interest of the public as he had from 1850 to 1852. The first edge of his popularity had worn off; he was not forgotten, but the first interest created by *The Scarlet Letter* and *The House of the Seven Gables* had gone. *The Blithedale Romance* did little to revive it; indeed, as we have said, it probably helped to smother the enthusiasm. The nature of its subject matter must have reminded the general public that Hawthorne after all belonged to a special circle, and may have suggested that Hawthorne could safely be left to the admiration of his friends. *The Scarlet Letter* was less talked of for having been so much talked of when it appeared. Hawthorne's fame was undergoing a necessary process of hibernation. America had other things to talk about; the magazines were turning more and more to political and social, rather than to literary, problems. We have a long gap in published comment until the publication of *The Marble Faun* brought a new crop of reviews, although there are a few items of interest.

We should mention Duyckinck's article in his *Cyclopaedia of American Literature*.[1] Duyckinck gives Hawthorne an important place in his collection of authors, and reprints " The Gray Champion " and " Sights from a Steeple " as examples of his work. His criticism is drawn almost entirely from the more general portions of his own notices including, however, only the more flattering phrases and ignoring that slight impatience with Hawthorne's " moonshine " which we have seen in his later comments. He gives an account of the progress of Hawthorne's literary reputation, with comments unfavorable to the American reading public. Hawthorne, he says, worked for twelve years without making any impression upon the public, though one or two of his pieces had a pretty wide newspaper circulation. But on the appearance of *The Scarlet Letter,* the public " was for once apprehensive, and the whole retinue of literary reputation makers

[1] Duyckinck, Evert A. and George L. *The Cyclopaedia of American Literature from the Earliest Period to the Present Day.* New York 1855 (2: 503–507).

fastened upon the genius of Hawthorne." Duyckinck does not give any indication of the comparative merit of the novels, discreetly remarking of *The House of the Seven Gables* that it is " one of the most elaborate and powerfully drawn of his later volumes," and of *The Blithedale Romance* that it is " one of the most original and inventive of the author's productions." With Duyckinck's article we might pair the biographical account of Hawthorne which appeared in 1859 in Allibone's *Dictionary of Authors*.[1] Hawthorne is there treated at respectful length. Allibone gives a sketch of his life, and follows it with a long and quite complete bibliography of critical notices. He quotes extensively from some of Hawthorne's critics, notably from Longfellow and Miss Mitford. In the same year there was another biography, in Edwin Paxton Hood's *Master Minds of the West*. It is based on Griswold and accompanied by selections from Hawthorne's works.[2]

Samuel Gilman, a genial Unitarian clergyman now better known for his song " Fair Harvard " than for his other verses or for his numerous prose writings, included in the *Contributions to Literature* which he printed in 1856 an essay said to have been written and published in 1838.[3] It is a humorous account of a pilgrimage to Salem undertaken by the writer in his capacity of fervent admirer of the *Twice-Told Tales*. There are also of course other scattered American references to Hawthorne during these years, like the one in Tuckerman's essay on Charles Brockden Brown,[4] which indicate that Hawthorne was uniformly considered of " classic " rank in American literature.

In England we find an article in *Tait's Edinburgh Magazine* for December 1856.[5] Hawthorne, the writer begins, belongs to a class of authors, few in number, who, not willing to be bound by laws of verse, allow their thoughts and feeling to mingle " with a flowing, easy and yet elevated style of prose." For Hawthorne is a poet in the

---

[1] Allibone, S. Austin. *A Critical Dictionary of English Literature and British and American Authors Living and Deceased, from the Earliest Accounts to the Middle of the Nineteenth Century.* Philadelphia 1859 (1: 804–806).
[2] Hood, Edwin Paxton. *Master Minds of the West.* London 1859.
[3] Gilman, Samuel. *Contributions to Literature.* Boston 1856. A Day of Disappointment in Salem. By an Admirer of Twice-Told Tales (pp. 474–496).
[4] Tuckerman, Henry T. *Essays, Biographical and Critical: or Studies of Character.* Boston 1857. Charles Brockden Brown (p. 377).
[5] *Tait's Edinburgh Magazine* (27:756–757) December 1856.

truest sense. "The depth, brilliancy and chasteness of his embellishments, when he takes in hand any commonplace incident or conventional prejudice, prove him to possess the highest poetical feeling, guarded by a refined and commanding intellect." He may be compared to Poe, the writer continues, but he is infinitely Poe's superior: "Possessed of many of Poe's qualities of genius, and happily free from the blemishes that taint his character, Hawthorne has produced fictions that are worthy of the foremost rank in our own language; and have been rarely equalled in any other." The writer goes on to commend, with illustrative quotations and in the most enthusiastic terms, Hawthorne's exquisite taste, delicacy of feeling and chivalrous attitude toward women.

This article, though it is apparently the only one of its kind, serves as a reminder that Hawthorne had a group of especial admirers in England—a fairly large group, but comparable in kind to the small group of the elect that had existed in America before the days of *The Scarlet Letter*. It consisted of persons interested in literature and possessed of "spiritual" tastes; and the fact that Hawthorne was comparatively unappreciated by the larger public made him the more dear to these few. During his residence in England Hawthorne was much lionized, and would have been much more so, if he had not passively and actively discouraged it.

The fact that Hawthorne was an American rather increased than diminished his reputation in England, at least among the *literati*. *Blackwood's* later pointed out, with some truth, that a distinguished foreign writer was likely to receive more honor of a certain kind than a native writer of equal merit and celebrity. As *Blackwood's* puts it: "His foreign extraction, his different breeding and the union of the strange and the familiar in his language and ideas, are what probably confers on his companionship, in the estimation of our social epicures, all the superiority of flavour which game possesses over poultry." [1] As an example of the kind of tribute Hawthorne received from his admirers, when he put himself in the way of it, one might cite the gushing letter of one of the Misses de Quincey, printed by Mrs. Ticknor.[2]

---

[1] *Blackwood's Magazine* (94: 610–623) November 1863. Hawthorne on England.

[2] See *Hawthorne and his Publisher*, pp. 83–84.

PART III

FROM THE MARBLE FAUN TO HAWTHORNE'S DEATH

AFTER years of silence Hawthorne again appeared before the public with *The Marble Faun,* or *Transformation,* as his English publishers insisted upon calling it. It was published in England at the end of February and in America early in March 1860.[1]

The first periodical to print a review was the *Athenaeum.*[2] Chorley is again the writer.

> Not with impunity can a novelist produce two such books—each, of its class, perfect—as *The Scarlet Letter* and *The House of the Seven Gables.* He is expected to go on: and his third and fourth romances will be measured by their predecessors, without reference to the fact that there may be slow growth and solitary perfection in the works of genius.

Chorley implies that most persons had been disappointed by Hawthorne's two latest novels; he himself does not express any definite opinion. He praises *Transformation* for its reflection of the beauty of Italy, and says that the spell of the South is so admirably rendered that the reader does not object to the suspension of the story. He praises the theme at least with the assertion that it is fearless; but the characters, he says, are disappointing in that they merely repeat characters in Hawthorne's previous novels. Miriam is Zenobia and Hilda is Phoebe, while Kenyon is "a stone image." Upon the subject of the conclusion of the story Chorley becomes emphatic. It is probably the most inconclusive and hazy ending in romance. He does not demand "a mathematical conclusion nor *coup de theatre* (as in the comedies of M. Scribe)" but he insists upon the necessity of a resolution of the emotional interest.

---

[1] *The Marble Faun,* or The Romance of Monte Beni. By Nathaniel Hawthorne, author of "The Scarlet Letter." Boston: Ticknor and Fields. 1860. 12mo., 2 vols., pp. 283–288.

[2] *Athenaeum* (pp. 296–297) March 3, 1860.

The review in the *Saturday Review* [1] is in much the same vein. The romance is a work of genius, it says, and genius is to some extent its own defence, although the work " not only tantalizes us by keeping us in a dim region of events that are neither probable nor improbable, neither possible nor impossible, but it defeats our expectations by sketching out a plot which comes absolutely to nothing." Hawthorne cheats the reader, who naturally assumes upon beginning a book that it will have an ending. The description is beautiful, the reviewer admits; and " however faulty the story as a story, it does undoubtedly produce the impression of mysterious horror that is so dear to Mr. Hawthorne."

The chief of Hawthorne's personal friends in England, Henry Bright, writing in the *Examiner*,[2] more mildly protested the mistiness of the ending, contrasting in general the formlessness of the book with the finish and definition of *The Scarlet Letter.* He praises *Transformation,* however, for its profound reflections upon the Fall of Man and for the delicacy with which the dangerous theme is treated; and he cannot sufficiently commend the beauty of the Roman descriptions or the charm of Hawthorne's style " which rises to a strain of thought or passion having in it a poetry like that which occurred sometimes in the first outpourings of De Quincey."

Hawthorne was so much distressed by these reviews and by private voices complaining about the conclusion that he hastily wrote out a brief final chapter for the book, though he was not able to provide a very satisfactory solution for a plot which, by its own nature and for artistic reasons, could end only as it began,—in a mist. The subsequent articles mostly deal with versions of the book which contain the additional chapter.

James Russell Lowell's review in the *Atlantic Monthly* for April is an excellent, though brief, criticism of Hawthorne's genius, very characteristic of Lowell.[3] It is now thirty years since Hawthorne's first appearance as an author, Lowell begins.

---

[1] *Saturday Review* (9: 341–342) March 17, 1860. Reprinted in *Littel's Living Age* (65: 323–325) May 12, 1860.

[2] *Examiner* (p. 197) March 31, 1860.

[3] *Atlantic Monthly* (5:509–510) April 1860.

His works have received that warranty of genius and originality in the widening of their appreciation downward from a small circle of refined admirers and critics, till it embraced the whole community of readers.

He continues, incidentally explaining his reason for coupling Shakespeare and Hawthorne in his later and more famous essay on Thoreau:

The nineteenth century has produced no more purely original writer than Mr. Hawthorne. A shallow criticism has sometimes fancied a resemblance between him and Poe, but it seems to us that the difference between them is the immeasurable one between talent carried to its ultimate, and genius—between a masterly adaptation of the world of sense and appearance to the purposes of Art, and a so thorough conception of the world of moral realities that Art becomes the interpreter of something profounder than herself. In this respect it is not extravagant to say that Hawthorne has something of kindred with Shakespeare. But that breadth of nature which made Shakespeare incapable of alienation from common human nature and actual human life is wanting to Hawthorne. He is rather a denizen than a citizen of what men call the world.

Hawthorne's works are abstract, Lowell says, and so they belong to the world and time, not to America and the present day; " it is their moral purpose alone, and perhaps their sadness, that mark him as the son of New England and the Puritans." His stories are all concentrated upon one point.

As in Rome the obelisks are placed at points toward which several streets converge, so in Mr. Hawthorne's stories the actors and incidents seem but vistas through which we see the moral from different points of view,—a moral pointing skyward always, but inscribed with hieroglyphs mysteriously suggestive, whose incitement to conjecture, while they baffle it, we prefer to any prosaic solution.

Hawthorne's characters are not alive " like Helen and Antigone and Benedick and Falstaff and Miranda, and Parson Adams, and Major Pendennis "; they are idiosyncrasies into which he has breathed a necromantic life. But if one grants him his premises, his creations are at once compelling and full of truth. Though Lowell does not specifically indicate that he prefers one of Hawthorne's works to another, he says of *The Marble Faun,* very truly:

In a series of remarkable and characteristic works, it is perhaps the most remarkable and characteristic. If you had picked up and read a stray leaf of it
anywhere, you would have exclaimed, " Hawthorne! "

The review by Charles Card Smith in the *North American
Review* [1] also contains a general tribute to Hawthorne's genius. His
characteristics, says Smith, are unchanged except " by modifications
arising from moral and intellectual growth." As a work of art he
is inclined to put *The Marble Faun* above Hawthorne's previous
books. Its style is warmer and its tone is more healthful. He likes
the contrast which Hawthorne distinctly makes between the " beautiful and sinless life of Hilda " and the " dark and guilt-stained career
of Miriam."

There is an article in the *Westminster Review* for April [2] (not by
the same hand as the previous *Westminster* comment) which praises
Hawthorne's originality and remarkable power of analysis as shown
in *Transformation,* and then proceeds to attack the book at every
point. Its thesis is too vaguely indicated; its characters are repeated
from *The Blithedale Romance* and besides are mere artificial opposites
of each other; its plot is faulty and its conclusion is baffling; and
finally, Hawthorne's choice of a Roman rather than a New England
scene was unfortunate. " These labored pictures of Italian skies, of
well known spots, of world renowned statues, and of some in American studios not yet so famous, have a strange flavour of the news
letter." *Transformation* is inferior to the other three novels, says
the reviewer, but in spite of that it is irresistibly attractive.

The *Times* [3] honored *Transformation* with a notice, which contained objections to the plot indeed, but which was on the whole extremely complimentary. Its tone of solemn felicitation was rightly
regarded by Hawthorne's friends as an extraordinary tribute, in view
of the fact that *Transformation* was, after all, written by an American.

For the May issue of the *Atlantic Monthly* [4] Edwin Percy Whipple
wrote a long essay called " Nathaniel Hawthorne," giving his final

[1] *North American Review* (90: 557–558) April 1860.
[2] *Westminster Review* (73: 624–627) April 1860.
[3] *The Times* (p. 5) April 7, 1860.
[4] *Atlantic Monthly* (5:614–622) May 1860.

opinion with great candor. In Hawthorne's early tales, he says, it is evident that the author had spiritual insight, without the ability to penetrate the sources of spiritual joy. This is the chief reason why his first work with all its beauties and with its excellent subject of life in New England, failed to attract public support. Hawthorne was interested, in an indolent way, in the conflict of ideas and passions, not in the individuals who embodied them.

In the romance of " The Scarlet Letter " he first made his genius efficient by penetrating it with passion. The book forced itself into attention by its inherent power; and the author's name, previously known only to a limited circle of readers, suddenly became a familiar word in the mouths of the great reading public of America and England. It may be said that it " captivated " nobody, but took everybody captive. . . . There were growls of disapprobation from novel readers, that Hester Prynne and the Rev. Mr. Dimmesdale were subjected to cruel punishments unknown to the jurisprudence of fiction, that the author was an inquisitor who put his victims on the rack—and that neither amusement nor delight resulted from seeing the contortions and hearing the groans of these martyrs of sin; but the fact was no less plain that Hawthorne had for once compelled the most superficial lovers of romance to submit themselves to the magic of his genius.

Hawthorne has a wonderful insight into spiritual laws, Whipple says, and he is merciless in exposing them. The austerest preacher of the Puritan church would have been kinder to Hester and Dimmesdale than Hawthorne. " Throughout ' The Scarlet Letter ' we seem to be following the guidance of an author who is personally good-natured but intellectually and morally relentless." *The House of the Seven Gables,* with less concentration and tension than *The Scarlet Letter,* includes a wider range of observation, reflection and character; but it would still be black if it were not for Phoebe, who radiates warmth and sunlight. Whipple is full of admiration for Phoebe. He remarks that the description of the Pyncheon poultry is unexcelled by anything in Dickens. Then he goes on to discuss his observation that Hawthorne's genius seems to be independent of his will. " He cannot use his genius; his genius always uses him." Returning to his orderly consideration of Hawthorne's works Whipple says of *The Blithedale Romance* that it is very characteristic of its author and a product of his peculiar method of shaping a piece of fiction. Hawthorne's mind apparently hits upon some moral idea and the idea gathers characters about it—characters whose reality depends upon the intensity of the mood out of which they came. *The Marble Faun,* " which must, on the whole, be considered the greatest of his works," proves that his genius has widened and deepened without changing its direction. The work has great value merely for its description of Italy and for its criticism of art. However the strictures which have been evoked by the plot are not unreasonable. Whipple perceptively points out that the plot is most defective in that it does not illustrate the theme very well. The murder of Miriam's persecutor, he says, does not seem like murder because the victim has no human traits. Whipple concludes by hoping that he has said nothing to give the impression that he does not consider Hawthorne's work to be " among the very highest productions of the age," and by, hoping that Hawthorne's mind will lose some of its sadness without losing any of its subtety and depth.

The following month we find an article of different tone in the *New Englander.*[1] Eliza Robbins, who occasionally wrote children's books and occasionally contributed an essay to one of the graver magazines, reviews *The Marble Faun* in a doubtful mood. She is disturbed by the characters in the book. As for the story it " is nothing but a reproduction of ' *The Scarlet Letter* ' save that the scene is transferred from New England to Italy." *The Marble Faun* is however better than *The Scarlet Letter,* and the reading public is a gainer by the transportation, for the description of Italy is beautiful and the criticism of art is valuable. Some of the sentiments which 'Hawthorne puts into the mouths of his characters, she notes, are dangerous in the extreme. She ends by quoting some commendation which Hawthorne had received, and by herself commending his style.

The larger volume of criticism continued to appear in England, where, indeed, the larger number of copies of the book were sold. The *Universal Review* has a long and carefully thought out article.[2] It begins (as do most of such articles in England) with generalities about American literature. America's most characteristic mode, the writer says, is humor; and in this field Lowell and Sam Slick are the

[1] *New Englander* (18: 441–452) May 1860.

[2] *Universal Review* (3: 742–771) June 1860. Nathaniel Hawthorne. Reprinted in *Littel's Living Age* (65: 707–723) June 23, 1860.

best representatives. In the serious vein, however, Hawthorne is the most national author that America has produced; for Hawthorne loves the legends of his country and reflects some of its transitional characteristics—the conflict between the material and the moral, the combination of " knowingness " and superstition. The writer undertakes to divide all of Hawthorne's works into three categories: I. Studies of historic events or everyday characters; II. Scenes and stories purely imaginative and fantastic; III. Allegories and moral sketches or narratives. He then abandons his classification (which, to be sure, is not very helpful) in order to discuss the works individually and in detail. He points out that there are two leading ideas in Hawthorne's writing. One of these motives may be expressed by the line of Persius which Kant took as a motto, *Tecum habita et noris quam sit tibi curta supellex*—that is to say, Hawthorne warns us against attempting to transcend in any way the conditions of our being. The other principal motive is the idea of secret guilt. The writer praises *The Scarlet Letter* and *The House of the Seven Gables*—the latter with the usual comparison to Dickens. He is less pleased with *The Blithedale Romance,* which has no central idea such as gives unity and force to the tales and to the two previous novels, and no plot as a substitute for an idea; and he says that *Transformation* shows a relaxation of nervous fiber. However " the brilliancy of style, the force of particular scenes and passages, and the general elegance of thought and imagination " make it remarkable. The essayist now returns to his principal idea—that of Hawthorne's nationalism. " He represents the *youthfulness* of America—not in respect of its physical vigour and energy, but of its vague aspirations, its curiosity, its syncretism, its strainings after the perception of psychologic mysteries, its transitory phases of exhausted cynicism, its tendency to the grotesque in taste and character, and its unscrupulous handling of some of the deepest secrets of our nature." The essay ends with a note upon Hawthorne's " powerful effects " and their tendency to morbidity, and with a hope that he will produce something more cheerful and varied in his next effort.

The *Dublin University Magazine* [1] has an essay of a lighter kind called " American Imaginings." It is written by someone who prides

---

[1] *Dublin University Magazine* (55: 679–688) June 1860.

himself upon his knowledge of Italy and consists largely of rambling comments on *Transformation* as a picture of Rome. The writer remarks with excessive amiability that British tourists are often almost as vulgar and ignorant as Yankee tourists, and then proceeds to agree in general with nearly all of Hawthorne's ideas, even with his praise of Story, even with his objection to the nude in art. He objects however to the character of Donatello and especially to " those pointed lynx ears, which Mr. Hawthorne's self set our fingers feeling for among mystic Tuscan's curls."

In August an essay appeared in the *North British Review* [1] with the title: " Imaginative Literature. The Author of Adam Bede and Nathaniel Hawthorne." It consists largely in a comparison between *The Mill on the Floss* and *Transformation*. The writer begins by speaking of the popular idea that imagination has an element of falseness in it.

One man has common sense,—another sees things as they are not. Such is the current phraseology;—the fact being that the man whose imagination is most intense and exalted, is the man whose impressions of things are, in general, the most truthful and exact. Doubtless there is a grain of truth in the popular view. The imagination in different men works under different laws. The more powerful intellects keep it in subjection, but it takes the feebler captive. In the one case, it vitalizes and exalts; in the other it discolours and exaggerates. The author of Adam Bede represents the first class; Nathaniel Hawthorne the second.

There follows a description and analysis of *The Mill on the Floss,* with numerous quotations. The comments dwell especially upon George Eliot's representation of character, upon her imaginative fidelity to life and upon the fact that she does not shrink from the prosaic. The writer especially admires her representation of childhood, which is, he points out, very different from that of Dickens in *Dombey and Son.* Some readers, the writer continues, will resent Hawthorne's ascription to the second class of imaginative writers. " The grave sympathy, the homely insight, the classic Puritanism, the rich and meditative intellect, have commended their owner to a multitude of admirers. . . . Nor can it be denied that his imagina-

---

[1] *North British Review* (33: 165–185) August 1860.

tion is vivid and affluent and capable of sustaining an impassioned and lofty flight. It is perhaps hardly fair, moreover, to assert without qualification that the imagination, which takes the colour of what it feeds on, is necessarily inferior." But it is undeniable, says the writer, that Hawthorne belongs to this class, whether it is first or second. At the moment he has been taken captive by the fascinations of Rome.

The writer now proceeds to compare Hawthorne and George Eliot in point of style.

Hers has a crystal-like purity; his is dyed with rich and varied colours. The rhetoric of *Adam Bede,* untouched by the heart or the imagination, might become bald; with these—exactly as we have it, in short—it is the perfection of natural eloquence. But even without original thought or deep feeling, Mr. Hawthorne's style—rich, fragrant and mixed with flowers of various hues, like Attic honey— would be always delightful.

But the true test, he continues, lies not in their style but in their relative power to delineate character; and there the evidence is decisive. In the one book character grows like a flower; in the other it is constructed like a machine. Hawthorne fits his characters into a prepared framework, thus sacrificing " the ease, *abandon,* and lawlessness of life." There is no life in *Transformation,* only a great deal of very delightful talk about life. The writer concludes by saying, as if in extenuation of his unfavorable comparison, that Hawthorne is nevertheless an admirable guide to Rome. He quotes a number of passages from *The Marble Faun* which deal with well known places and works of art.

This able and interesting essay is the first and last complete expression of what has since come to be known as realistic criticism, though a previous article has hinted at it, as we have said. The points it makes are irreproachable and sound in view of the principles from which they are deduced—principles whose gradual emergence into popular consciousness has in later times contributed to the decline, if not of Hawthorne's reputation, then of his influence at least. But as a piece of absolute criticism it is of course open to objections. It is unfair to compare *The Mill on the Floss* and *The Marble Faun* because (aside from other considerations) they belong to different kinds of writing and they serve different purposes. Hawthorne and George Eliot were both labeled " psychological novelists " in the critical jargon of the period; but they were psychological with a difference and they were working with different materials. Richard Holt Hutton's article in the *National Review* for October [1] is in this respect more just and sympathetic. It is, indeed, the best piece of criticism which had so far appeared, in its perception, its original reflections, and its sympathy.

Hutton begins his article by remarking that Hawthorne desires to obtain a special moonlight effect in his writings. He illustrates this point by excerpts from Hawthorne's prefaces. The phrase " the moonlight of romance," he continues, is applicable to Hawthorne in that his characters are, not unreal, but revealed in a special light. Hawthorne's novels are not novels in the ordinary sense, but detailed treatments of ideal situations. All of Hawthorne's narratives, says Hutton, embody single ideal situations—that is, single ideas. The novels might have been tales without loss of incident. But the minute care of their elaboration is not wasted; the secret of Hawthorne's power lies in the great art with which the main idea is reflected and reduplicated until the reader is saturated and haunted by it. In Hawthorne's case allegory is not the sign of a meager and shallow imagination; for the longer he broods over his ideas the more substance and variety they gain. Poe was mistaken in thinking Hawthorne's allegorizing was the hall-mark of a clique; it is natural and necessary to his talent.

Hutton remarks upon the contrast between the simplicity of the incidents in Hawthorne's writing and the complexity of the emotions.

We might almost say he has carried into human affairs the old Calvinistic type of imagination. The same strange combination of clear simplicity, high faith and reverential reality, with the reluctant but for that reason intense and devouring conviction of the large comprehensiveness of the Divine Damnation which that grim creed taught its most honest believers to consider true trust in God's providence, Mr. Hawthorne copies into human life.

That is, says Hutton, Hawthorne describes the process by which one idea encroaches on, and gradually absorbs, everything else. The

[1] *National Review* (11: 453–481) October 1860. Reprinted in *Littel's Living Age* (68: 211–213) January 26, 1861.

emotions depicted, though subtle and unhealthy, are justified by the power of their treatment. Hutton here gives an admirable description of *The Scarlet Letter* and of *The Marble Faun,* remarking incidentally that Hawthorne, unlike Poe, is not interested in monsters and horrors, but in the struggle between opposing moral forces.

The bent of Hawthorne's genius, Hutton continues, is inquisitive rather than ardent. Upon the subject of Hawthorne's plots he makes a reflection that seems simple enough and yet one that had not presented itself to any other critic. Hawthorne suppresses distinct events, he says, as dangerous to the reader's sympathy: for one might think mental anguish resulting from a slight offense silly, and from a heavy offense deserved. Hawthorne is interested only in portraying states of mind; and the tenuousness of his construction is necessary and natural. Hutton remarks however that too much absence of fact (as in *Transformation*) is unsatisfactory. " *The Scarlet Letter,* in which there is by far the most solid basis of fact, is, we think, considerably the finest and most powerful of his effects." Hutton concludes his essay by pointing out Hawthorne's want of sympathy not only with " the world of voluntary action " but with " the world of impulsive passion." Hawthorne, he says, has a bias toward *chronic* states of suffering or sentiment, a kind of fatalism which mars an otherwise noble morality. This fatalism may be justifiable as applied to the reformatory spirit in *The Blithedale Romance* but " when it is applied to the actual political world in which he lives, we see his moral shortcomings." There follows a reference to the *Life of Franklin Pierce* and an eloquent diatribe against the slavery interests, which *Littel's Living Age,* in reprinting the article, discreetly omitted.

To conclude our list of English references for the year 1860 we might mention an article in *The Crayon* [1] which consists largely of a translation (not entirely accurate) of the most brilliant and certainly the least impugnable passage in Emile Montegut's essay in the *Revue des Deux Mondes*—the informed, just, and very unEnglish

---

[1] *The Crayon* (7: 299–301) October 1860.

and unAmerican comment upon Hawthorne's artistic judgment.[1] We might compare this comment of Montegut's with one that Hawthorne's lion-hunting acquaintance Samuel Carter Hull had printed in his *Art-Journal*.[2] In the *Art-Journal* notice we learn that Hall liked nothing in the book but the artistic criticism, which he considered not only delightful but original and highly instructive. We might note that *The Crayon* apparently does not understand in the least the criticism which it is quoting, and regards the passage in Montegut's article merely as justified disapprobation of Hawthorne's "puffs" of American artists. We should also mention that Hawthorne found another biographer in this year in the person of Samuel Smiles, the celebrated apostle of self help.[3]

Hawthorne's ardent English admirers took his new romance warmly and seriously into their hearts. One of them [4] was moved to compose a poem upon the subject of *The Marble Faun*. The poem describes Rome as inspiring genius by her awful beauty; and then goes on to speak of the lofty moral meaning of the book:

> " From evils, goods,—from sin and sorrow, peace,
>   A holier future, and a loftier faith."—
>   This to my soul thy mystic volume saith,
>   Hawthorne, and bids doubt's spectral night to cease. . . .

As a representative of Hawthorne's American enthusiasts we might cite Motley, who wrote Hawthorne a graceful and interesting letter on the subject of his new romance. (He had made Hawthorne's acquaintance when they were in Rome together.) He is vain, he

---

[1] *Revue des Deux Mondes* (28:668–703) August 1, 1860. Montegut, Emile. Un Romancier Pessimiste en Amerique. Nathaniel Hawthorne. In this article (which is interesting throughout although open to the objection that, like much excellent French criticism, it is too precise and centered too closely upon one idea) Montegut explains that the weakness of Hawthorne's artistic judgment lies, not in lack of sensibility, but in lack of extended acquaintance with art. In this field, he says, a European child, a child not even very gifted or perceptive, could set Hawthorne right. A European, simply because he has the advantage of being accustomed to the sight of great works of art, could tell Hawthorne that his preference for artists of the third or fourth rank (for Guido Reni for instance) comes from the fact that such artists court one's regard by obvious tricks, while the great artists earn it by validity of conception and solidity of workmanship.

[2] *Art-Journal* (p. 127) April 1, 1860.

[3] Smiles, Samuel. *Brief Biographies*. London 1860. Nathaniel Hawthorne (pp. 257–269).

[4] William Bennett. See *Nathaniel Hawthorne and his Wife* (2:253–254).

writes,[1] of having admired " Sights from a Steeple " when he saw it in the *Token* " several hundred years ago " and of having detected and cherished " The Old Apple Dealer." He admires *The Marble Faun* immensely:

> Where, oh where is the godmother who gave you to talk pearls and diamonds? How easy it seems until anybody else tries! Believe me, I don't say to you half what I say behind your back; and I have said a dozen times that nobody can write English but you. I like those shadowy, weird, fantastic Hawthornesque shapes flitting through the golden gloom which is the atmosphere of the book. I like the misty way in which the story is indicated rather than revealed. The outlines are quite definite enough, from the beginning to the end, to those who have imagination enough to follow you in your airy flights; and to those who complain, I suppose nothing less than an illustrated edition, with Donatello in the most pensive of attitudes, his ears revealed at last through a white night-cap, would be satisfactory.

The Civil War was now beginning; and the issues of the struggle occupied men's minds and forced literary issues into the background. In 1861 we find only one article, an attempt to dissipate the " obscurity " of *The Marble Faun* by the use of an intricate system of allegory.[2] It was written by Mrs. Martha Tyler Gale, and, when reprinted in 1892, was headed by a note saying that the article had been read and approved by Hawthorne. This is not improbable in view of Hawthorne's character; he would have smiled and passively consented. And as a matter of fact the allegory is very ingenious. Miriam is Soul; Hilda is Conscience; Kenyon is Reason; and Donatello is Nature. The monk is Temptation. In these terms the narrative can be worked out very neatly, and it is even possible to explain the much criticized conclusion. For instance, Hilda's deliverance of the papers to the Roman authorities, her mysterious imprisonment and mysterious release are accounted for thus: " Conscience keeps the moral accounts of the soul, and will present them sooner or later at the tribunal of justice. But Conscience herself becomes morbid, and is often brought under bondage to superstition, while sin remains unpunished or unpardoned."

---

[1] See *Memories of Hawthorne*, pp 406–410.

[2] *New Englander* (19: 860–870) October 1861. The Marble Faun, with a Key to its Interpretation. Reprinted in the *New Englander* (56: 26–36) January 1892.

This silence upon the theme of Hawthorne's works, if one excepts the comments on *Our Old Home,* lasted indeed until 1864. The only critical article which we find in these intervening years is an under-graduate essay in the *Yale Literary Magazine.*[1] This is distinguished by a staccato style and by a lyric appreciation of Hawthorne's powers. " Who that has read the ' Scarlet Letter,' " asks the writer, " will ever forget the livid portrayal of guilt; secret, yet unconcealable guilt? "

Were the workings of sin ever more perfectly idealized into character? A heavy oppression of guilt lies like a leaden mountain upon the soul. The secret of blood forever haunts the conscience. An unconfessed war is waged with society. The same deep-coloured, mysterious thread runs through the Marble Faun, the same heavy spirited being wearing away life under some unexpressed care and deep-hidden remorse. The Scarlet Letter, though physically unseen, flames in the heart of the walking mystery. This is delineated with masterly touches.

The essayist remarks that a great moral underlies Hawthorne's ro-mances. " The lesson is continually taught," he writes, " that moral truth is sure to triumph because it has a friend in man's own heart."

As an indication of Hawthorne's established status we might men-tion the *Handbook of Universal Literature* compiled by the then well known poetess and friend of literature, Anna Lynch Botta.[2] The section on American literature is brief (necessarily, in an account which surveys all literature, including the Oriental and the Slavic) but it is noticeable that Hawthorne is treated at greater length than any other American author. Hawthorne is remarkable, says Mrs. Botta, for his psychological insight, his power of intense characteriza-tion and his mastery of the spiritual and the supernatural. He is most at home in dark subjects, she adds. As an indication of Haw-thorne's serious reputation as a " philosopher of the heart " we might mention an essay by Francis Jacox[3] which discusses the ethical prob-lem proposed by " Fancy's Show-Box."

---

[1] *Yale Literary Magazine* (28: 300–303) June 1863.
[2] Botta, Anne Lynch. *Handbook of Universal Literature.* Boston 1863 (p. 530).
[3] *Bentley's Miscellany* for 1863. Jacox, Francis. Imperfect Criminals. A Vexed Question.

When Hawthorne published " Chiefly about War Matters " in the *Atlantic Monthly* there was some private comment of no very acrimonious kind, for all that its tone was curiously at variance with the temper of the times in New England. His acquaintances were convinced that Hawthorne was politically incorrigible; and they were even inclined to believe that the detachment of his point of view was a quality of the poetic temperament. The article, being anonymous, occasioned no such newspaper notices as the *Life of Franklin Pierce*.

Our Old Home attracted very little public attention in America, either when it was running in the form of separate papers through the *Atlantic Monthly* or when it was published in book form in September 1863.[1] Emerson, however, said with his usual originality that " Recollections of a Gifted Woman " was the best thing that Hawthorne ever wrote.[2] There were few American notices and those were brief. The *North American Review*[3] said that the chief interest of the sketches was autobiographical—a delightful revelation of Hawthorne's humor and kindliness. Upon the more " political " side we find a note in the *Continental Monthly*[4] which praises " these truthful and agreeable sketches " for their balanced attitude and their quiet patriotism; and remarks that the chapter on English poverty may be regarded as a warning to us.

In England the reception of *Our Old Home* was quite different. It attracted a great deal of notice and that principally of the most unfavorable sort.

The *Reader,* for instance, after first reprinting a long series of extracts from the volume,[5] published a leading article full of savage abuse and equally savage self-felicitation.[6] The editorial writer accepts Hawthorne's remark about the beefy qualities in English character as an inverted compliment to the mental solidity and integrity of England; and after hurling Shakespeare, Bacon, Milton and Nelson at Hawthorne's head, observes that American rancor arises

---

[1] *Our Old Home.* A Series of English Sketches. By Nathaniel Hawthorne. Boston: Ticknor and Fields. 1863. 12mo., pp. 398.
[2] Conway's *Life*, pp. 98–99. See also Emerson's *Journals* (9: 90).
[3] *North American Review* (97: 588–589) October 1863.
[4] *Continental Monthly* (4: 595) November 1863.
[5] *Reader* (2:336–338) September 26, 1863. Reprinted in *Littel's Living Age* (79: 243–250) November 7, 1863.
[6] Ibid. (2:367–368) October 3, 1863.

from jealousy—a jealousy particularly marked, he gloatingly concludes, now that " it seems possible that their grandiose dream of a great and united American nation is about to be disappointed." However the *Spectator* a few days later has an article in a different vein,[1] from the civilized and unconventional pen of Richard Hutton. Hutton impishly wishes that Hawthorne had indulged in more racy remarks about the English. He even approves of the shocking comments on Englishwomen, while taking occasion to quote, in silent reproof of the injustice of the storm aroused by one passage, some more complimentary passages of a similar kind. He thinks Hawthorne's humor delicious, he says, and is disposed to quarrel with him, if at all, upon party grounds—upon the fact that he has not repented of writing the *Life of Pierce*. And in the *Examiner* [2] Henry Bright, while mildly protesting some of his friend's opinions (he protested more strongly by letter), points out the beauty of the description and says that it is better, because less artificial, than Irving's.

The worst of the notices appeared in *Punch*,[3] where we find, under the title " A Handful of Hawthorn," a positively gibbering cry of rage and hatred. The article in *Blackwood's* [4] is more in sorrow than in anger. *Our Old Home* is regarded as one unmitigated insult, the less bearable because it comes from an author whom England has delighted to honor. And justly delighted to honor, says the reviewer, in that his work is not merely " a clear and harmonious rendering of strange combinations of ideas " but contains a felicity of observation and clarity of style recalling " the simple yet subtle charm with which Addison and Goldsmith and Irving wrote." The reviewer follows this tribute with ten pages of quotations from *Our Old Home* and with laments for " such foolish denunciations." He regards Hawthorne as an abolitionist and heaps upon him all the disapproval which he feels for the Federal cause, even interpreting one sentence in the book (Hawthorne's remark that McClellan might have got to Richmond by shutting one eye) as an infamous proposal for fostering a servile insurrection.

---

[1] *Spectator* (36:2578–2580) October 3, 1863.

[2] *Examiner*, October 17, 1863.

[3] *Punch* (45:161). Reprinted in *Littel's Living Age* (79:339–340) November 21, 1863.

[4] *Blackwood's Magazine* (94: 610–623) November 1863. Partially reprinted in *Littel's Living Age* (80: 15–16).

This article was followed by a heavy-handed denunciation in the *Times,*[1] by a long essay in the *Christian Remembrancer*[2] which implies that Hawthorne's opinions were dictated by national prejudices, though it professes admiration rather than anger, and by an elaborate article in the *Quarterly Review,*[3] of the most John Bullish sort, in which *Our Old Home* is compared with Emerson's *English Traits* with conclusions not very favorable to either observer and most unfavorable to their country.

The controversy over *Our Old Home* has not much significance in the story of Hawthorne criticism. The issues were national rather than literary or personal. The period of the Civil War is a most unfortunate chapter in the history of Anglo-American relations. How unpleasant it was, for an American living in England, is succinctly told by Henry Adams in his *Education;* and a great number of political incidents bear witness at once to the force and to the irrationality of the torrent of British feeling against the Northern cause. *Our Old Home* appeared at a critical time and—any stick will do to beat a dog—it drew upon itself a portion of the popular rage. Hawthorne himself was much surprised by the furore, for he had fancied, with some reason, that his recorded impressions of England were just and even flattering; and he was now so remote from the current of English life (if indeed he had ever been in it) that he did not realize the denunciation arose as much from the crisis in affairs as from British insistence upon abject flattery. However the three articles which are generally approving (those in the *Spectator,* the *Examiner* and the *Christian Remembrancer*) remind us not only that the North retained some friends in England, but that Hawthorne lost none of his admirers by his frankness. They may have been piqued by his comments, but they were not inclined to lower their estimate of his talent.

In the meanwhile Hawthorne had been working with failing health and failing powers upon a new romance, or rather, upon a number of sketches for romances. The first chapter of one of these

---

[1] *Times* (p. 10) November 9, 1863.
[2] *Christian Remembrancer* (47: 165–188) January 1864. Reprinted in *Littel's Living Age* (81: 99–114) April 16, 1864.
[3] *Quarterly Review* (115: 42–68) January 1864. New Englanders and the Old Home. Reprinted in *Littel's Living Age* (80: 339–353) February 20, 1864.

was published soon after his death in the *Atlantic Monthly,* but Hawthorne found himself unable to continue. His health continued to fail; and he died May 20, 1864, while on a trip with Franklin Pierce. He was buried in Concord, with a group of New England's most eminent men as mourners—Emerson, Longfellow, Holmes, Agassiz, Hoar, Dwight, Whipple, Norton, Alcott, Hillard and Fields. Emerson gives an account of the funeral in his journal, adding a few lines which are interesting both for the light they throw upon the personal relations of the two men and upon Emerson's final estimate of Hawthorne's writing.[1]

I have found in his death a surprise and disappointment. I thought him a greater man than any of his works betray, that there was still a great deal of work in him, and that he might one day show a purer power. Moreover I have felt sure of him in his neighborhood, and in his necessities of sympathy and intelligence,—that I could wait his time,—his unwillingness and caprice,—and might one day conquer a friendship. It would have been a happiness, doubtless to both of us, to have come into habits of unrestranied intercourse. It was easy to talk to him,—there were no barriers,—only, he said so little, that I talked too much, and stopped only, as he gave no indications, I feared to exceed. He showed no egotism or self assertion, rather a humility, and, at one time, a fear that he had written himself out. One day when I found him on the top of his hill, in the woods, he paced back the path to his house, and said, " This path is the only remembrance of me that will remain." Now it appears that I waited too long.

Lately he had removed himself the more by the indignation his perverse politics and unfortunate friendship for that paltry Franklin Pierce awakened, though it rather moved pity for Hawthorne, and the assured belief that he would outlive it, and come right at last.

Emerson is here returning to the thought which he had held from the beginning of Hawthorne's career to its end—that Hawthorne himself was superior to his writing. But in respect that he expresses surprise and disappointment he is giving voice to a general sentiment. Hawthorne's serious readers were mostly devotees, and they felt his loss as if it were that of a personal friend. The members of what may be called the larger New England group, who, with whatever differences of opinion, had regarded Hawthorne as one of their peculiar glories, were broken hearted.

---

[1] See his *Journals* (10: 39–41).

Henry Bright wrote a graceful obituary essay upon his friend in the *Examiner*.[1] He speaks of his personal loss, and then proceeds to speak of the loss to literature. "We have in the old country," he says, "two or three novelists of genius as true, and one with higher gifts than Hawthorne's; but neither here nor in America is there any writer to fill the place which stands vacant now, and that borderland between prose and poetry, which he made his own, now lies unclaimed by any."

Oliver Wendell Holmes, writing an introduction to the scene from *The Dolliver Romance* which was published in the *Atlantic Monthly* in July,[2] gives an account of Hawthorne's last illness and of his funeral; and then proceeds to pay an eloquent tribute to his genius. Hawthorne, he says, was a poet although he did not write in verse. The present selection is worthy of the hand of the dead master.

That limpid flow of expression, never laboring, never shallow, never hurried, nor uneven, nor turgid, but moving on with tranquil force, clear to the depths of its profoundest thought, shows itself with all its consummate perfections. Our literature could ill spare the rich ripe autumn of such a life as Hawthorne's, but he has left enough to keep his name in remembrance as long as the language in which he shaped his deep imaginations is spoken by human lips.

This brief essay together with the fragment it introduces was printed soon afterward in London as a kind of memorial volume, under the title of *Pansie*.[3]

Edward Dicey, an English pilgrim who had made Hawthorne's acquaintance in 1861, wrote a sympathetic and revealing study of Hawthorne's character in *Macmillan's Magazine* for July;[4] and Richard Hutton returned to the consideration of Hawthorne in the *Spectator*, in a somewhat different vein than that of his previous article.[5] Hutton's interests were more theological than literary, and Hawthorne's death set him speculating upon the relation between his writing and the old New England Calvinism. His own background

---

[1] *Examiner*, June 18, 1864. Nathaniel Hawthorne's Death. Reprinted in *Littel's Living Age* (82: 222) July 30, 1864.

[2] *Atlantic Monthly* (14:98–101) July 1864.

[3] Hawthorne, Nathaniel. Pansie, His Last Literary Effort. London 1864.

[4] *Macmillan's Magazine* (10:241–246) July 1864.

[5] *Spectator* (37:705–706) July 18, 1864. Reprinted in *Littel's Living Age* (82: 219–222) July 30, 1864. This article appears with very little change in Hutton, R. H. Essays Theological and Literary. London 1871 (2: 370–374).

was Unitarian; and he was well qualified to speak upon the subject. He begins by saying that Hawthorne has been called a mystic, which he was not, and a psychological dreamer, which he was in a very slight degree. But really, he continues, Hawthorne was the ghost of New England—using the word ghost in the older sense of a thin rarefied essence which is found behind a physical organization. " His writings are not exactly spiritual writings; for there is no dominating spirit in them. They are ghostly writings." Hawthorne, says Hutton, is a sign of the divorce which is occurring in New England between its people's spiritual and earthly nature, and of the impotence which they will soon feel, if they are to be absorbed more and more in materialism, in communicating with the ghost of their former self. Hawthorne is unable to communicate with the world in an unreserved way. His mysteries (here Hutton returns in a more general way to a point made in his former article) are not intended to mystify; they are owing to the author's fear that by being definite he will convey not his own conception, but something different and inconsistent. Hawthorne regrets that his country has no past, says Hutton, but it is not the past he yearns for; it is for some interposing film—some excuse for the far off and distant tone which was natural to him. Poe was wrong (here Hutton again returns to a thought expressed previously) in advising Hawthorne to create prehensible and comprehensible literature.

> That pallid, tender, solitary, imaginative treatment of characteristics and problems which have lain and still lie, very close to the heart of New England—that power of exhibiting them lit up by the moonlight of a melancholy imagination, that ghostly half appeal for sympathy, half offer of counsel on the diseases latent in the New England nature—were no eccentricity, but the essence of his literary power.

Hutton returned to the subject of Hawthorne later in the year, in a review of *Pansie* [1] which is really an addition to this article. He speaks of the beauty of Hawthorne's style, rarely rivaled either in England or in America, although a classical simplicity and refinement has distinguished almost all the greater authors of America. He says that the *Dolliver* fragment is characteristic in this respect.

---

[1] *Spectator* (pp. 1075-1076) September 17, 1864. Mr. Hawthorne's Last Fragment. Reprinted in *Littel's Living Age* (83: 147-149) October 22, 1864.

There is in every sentence a silvery beauty, which Hawthorne himself has seldom equalled. It is curious that by far the most original of American literary men strikes us so often both in style and substance, as nearer the classical standard of English authors than any Englishman we could produce. New England has filtered away much of the richness and also much of the impurity of Anglo-Saxon genius. There is something exquisitely delicate, but refined away almost to gossamer, in the tissue of the noblest genius of the New World.

These two articles, Dicey's and Hutton's, are the most remarkable of those brought forth by Hawthorne's death—the one for its interesting portrait, which gives an insight into Hawthorne's character much like that given by his own journals and note-books, and the other for its original reflections. That they are both English illustrates again the advantage of a certain detachment in place. Hutton's ideas may not be correct in their entirety, but they represent intellectual effort brought to bear upon a new problem; while most of Hawthorne's American critics, even the most eminent, are content to repeat, with more or less effusion, what has been said before—to pick out of the current critical vocabulary an assortment of appropriate phrases and put them together, with suitable qualifications, into essays. It is not unfair to compare Hutton with Longfellow and Lowell and Whipple, for he belonged in general to their school of thought. Though advanced in his political thinking he was no proponent of the newer school in literature—no " realist " that is to say—and his judgment, like theirs, was based upon a sympathy with the older, rather than the newer, masterpieces of English literature. And Dicey had the advantage of meeting Hawthorne without preconceptions. He was not hampered in his judgment by the legend current in America (where indeed it was justified by Hawthorne's essential lack of sympathy with the ideas and the persons of his immediate circle) that Hawthorne was an unapproachable recluse, meditating in secret upon dark thoughts and poetic fancies. The two articles are more or less contradictory in that Dicey represents Hawthorne as human and Hutton calls him a ghost, but they are not contradictory beyond possibility of reconciliation, for they both contain elements of truth and perception.

George William Curtis' tribute, spoken from his " Editor's Easy Chair " in August,[1] emphasizes Hawthorne's native qualities.

---

[1] *Harper's Magazine* (29: 405) August 1864. Editor's Easy Chair.

In original genius no name in our literature is superior to his; and while everybody was asking whether it were impossible to write an American novel he wrote romances that were hardly possible elsewhere, because they were so purely American. . . . It [his genius] was not a growth of the English or the German or the French; nor was it eclectic. It was American. It was almost New England, except for the universality which belongs to such genius, and which made the "Marble Faun" no less a characteristic work of Hawthorne's than the "Scarlet Letter."

In the same month Longfellow published in the *Atlantic Monthly* his poem on Hawthorne's death.[1] It describes Hawthorne's funeral with the beauty and the sensibility which are characteristic of its composer, and ends with an expression of the common and the justified feeling of irreparable loss.

> There in seclusion and remote from men
>   The wizard hand lies cold,
> Which at its topmost speed let fall the pen,
>   And left the tale half told.
>
> Ah, who shall lift that wand of magic power,
>   And the lost clue regain?
> The unfinished window in Aladdin's tower
>   Unfinished must remain.

In August in *Fraser's Magazine* we find that Moncure Daniel Conway, writing wittily upon "The Transcendentalists of Concord,"[2] includes a passage upon Hawthorne in which he speaks briefly (as he was later to speak at length) of Hawthorne's separation from the world and of his mysterious character. The same qualities are dwelt upon in the most elaborate article of the year, and the last one to appear—George William Curtis' essay "The Works of Nathaniel Hawthorne."[3] It is a rambling biographical sketch, embodying much of the material presented in *Homes of American Authors* and adding more, especially in regard to Hawthorne's residence in Salem. He

---

[1] *Atlantic Monthly* (14: 169–170) August 1864. Longfellow, Henry W. Concord.

[2] *Fraser's Magazine* (70:245–264) August 1864. Reprinted in *Littel's Living Age* (83: 99–105) October 15, 1864.

[3] *North American Review* (99:539–557) October 1864. Also in Curtis, George W. Literary and Social Essays. New York 1895 (pp. 61–98).

says incidentally that *The Marble Faun* is " one of the most perfect
works of art in literature." He much prefers it to *The Scarlet
Letter,* which is forcible, he indicates, but too livid and too unre-
lieved. He speaks of his personal regard for Hawthorne, and ends
by felicitating himself and all of Hawthorne's friends in that the
name of Nathaniel Hawthorne " is now one of the most enduring
facts of English literature." The principal emphasis of the article,
however, lies upon the elusive and retiring aspects of Hawthorne's
character. The impression conveyed is that Hawthorne was a
romantic recluse of a poetical temperament so fine and sensitive that
he shrank almost from the mere light of day. The portrait drawn
is more or less the conventional one of a poet haunted by his dream.
This conception of Hawthorne's character was not invented by
Curtis (nor indeed was it entirely invented, for it is based upon truth
in a certain measure), but it is worth noticing that Curtis was one
of the earliest promoters of the Hawthorne " legend " and one of its
most consistent supporters. The legend indubitably affected some of
the contemporaneous criticism of Hawthorne; and it was very persistent in after years, lending its own somewhat artificial interest to
the interest in his writings. Woodberry contented himself by silently
correcting this very common conception; while Brownell protested
against it with embittered vigor. There was some justification in his
annoyance, for a misconception of this sort increases in force and in
degree of error as its subject grows more remote.

As a final addition to the list of comments on Hawthorne in this
year of his death we should mention Alexander Smith's *Dreamthorp*.[1]
In the essay called " A Shelf in My Bookcase " he lists *Twice-Told
Tales* among the books, none of them by the greatest authors, which
he has singled out as, so to speak, his intimate friends. He prefers
Twice-Told Tales, he says, to *Transformation* and *The Scarlet
Letter,* works by which the world at large sets more store, because
they were written for the author, while the novels were written for
the world. He is delighted by their revelation of the author's peculiar
and delightful character; and he chooses as his especial favorites such
pieces as " Sunday at Home," " Night Sketches," " Footprints on

---

[1] Smith, Alexander. *Dreamthorp.* London 1864. A Shelf in My Bookcase (pp. 191–212).

the Seashore" and "The Seven Vagabonds." This last, he says, "seems to me almost the most exquisite thing which has flowed from its author's pen." Smith is impressed by Hawthorne's skill in constructing allegories, and he delights in the hidden meaning of the tales. His comments remind one very much of Peabody (in respect to his first article at least) and of Longfellow. Smith is of course in this essay making a display of his mild eccentricities of a retiring lover of literature, but his professed preferences are nevertheless sincere. They call attention to the fact that there were hearts in Great Britain as well as in America which delighted especially in Hawthorne's meditative fancies and simple allegories.

In respect that Smith classifies Hawthorne as not among "the greatest authors" he is not expressing the sentiments of Hawthorne's American readers, or of his especial admirers abroad. George William Curtis is reporting a popular verdict when he says that Hawthorne's name is "among the most enduring facts of English literature." At the time of Hawthorne's death no one, in America at least, questioned his classic status. Curtis is also reporting a popular verdict when he says, or implies, that *The Marble Faun* is Hawthorne's greatest work. The majority of Hawthorne's readers agreed with him; and the agreement remained in force for a long time. Henry James said in 1879 that it was probably the most popular of Hawthorne's novels; and the tendency to exalt it to the position of "one of the most perfect works of art in literature" continued at least until the end of the century—that is to say, until there was a general and major change in taste. For *The Marble Faun*, beyond Hawthorne's other works, appealed especially to the taste of the period—not to popular taste to be sure, but to the predilections of the class which had made Hawthorne's writings its own.

None of Hawthorne's writings, during his lifetime, made as deep an impression as *The Scarlet Letter*, but this impression was owing partly, as we have said, to other considerations than those admitted by his appreciative critics. Its force and originality made itself felt as it were involuntarily; and its "dangerous" theme, however coldly and obliquely treated, gave it, in the absence of other reputable representations of such subjects, a special impact—a certain notoriety not evoked by the other works. The usual critical judgment was to place *The House of the Seven Gables* above *The Scarlet Letter;* and then to place *The Marble Faun* above both. The reasons for this have been apparent. And as a matter of fact Hawthorne's own judgment coincided with the verdict of the day. He insisted that *The House of the Seven Gables* was better than *The Scarlet Letter* as well as "more characteristic of my mind and more proper and natural for me to write"; and he said of *The Marble Faun* that, if he had written anything well, it was this romance.

A FEW WORDS IN CONCLUSION

THE opinions which have been quoted in the course of this study speak for themselves. To attempt to summarize them in any rigorous fashion would be to distort their meaning. Collectively they present an impression of the manner in which Hawthorne was regarded by his contemporaries; and they give some insight into the tastes and the critical principles of the day, at least as they were held by representative and eminent members of the cultivated classes. For although most of the material which we have presented consists of notices and reviews from periodicals, the notices and reviews are in general much above the average standard of the present day. A large portion of the American notices were written by persons who were distinguished in the field of letters. The English notices fall more generally into the category of "professional reviewing," but even there we find many instances of interesting and thoughtful writing. And it is worth noting that, in America at least, we find representatives of nearly all the departments of thought that were then flourishing. The transcendental point of view appears in Dr. Loring's article; and Lowell and Longfellow and Whipple variously represent the point of view of that larger portion of the New England group which was not transcendental. The religious view is represented as it ranged through different shades of belief from Catholic to advanced Unitarian. The professional world of letters is diversely represented by Benjamin and Hoffman and Poe. The unspecialized point of view—the common sense attitude, one might say—is represented, at least in its appreciative aspect, by Duyckinck.

Aside from the doctrinal or social alliances of the critics we have attempted here and there to distinguish the kinds of criticism which Hawthorne's work evoked, though without drawing any impracticable sharp distinctions. The terms employed—impressionistic, romantic, classical, realistic—are neither very expressive nor very consonant with each other; but they do serve the purpose of indicating certain groups of opinions. We might here add another term to our list, namely ethical criticism; and we should note that it is an important type though we have not previously given it a name.

Ethical criticism (which considers chiefly the moral aim of a writer and the moral effect of his writings upon the reader) formed a large part of the contemporaneous comment upon Hawthorne; and ethical considerations colored almost the whole of the discussion of his works, and gave rise to the chief differences of opinion. This was quite natural not only in view of the preoccupations of the period but in view of the character of Hawthorne's writing, which has simply no other subject than the soul. The verdict arrived at depended upon the convictions of the critic. Hawthorne won the regard of the conservative and orthodox critics by his early works only to be the more earnestly reprehended after the appearance of *The Scarlet Letter;* while the liberals, the post-Calvinistic believers, were for the most part inclined to praise his later works above his earlier ones, for their greater profundity. Though with reservations: for light scepticism and fanciful speculation displayed in the treatment of subject matter which was strictly limited to Calvinistic problems, was a hard moral nut to crack. Hawthorne's peculiar and specialized interest in the grave questions of the older New England theology, anachronistic in a day when the world no longer felt their urgency although it had not altogether come to doubt their validity, gave even his most liberal and sympathizing critics a feeling that his writing was too gloomy to be quite healthful; and in some quarters, not necessarily orthodox, gave his temperament the wholly undeserved reputation of being positively malign and insalubrious.

One may ask finally: how did the criticisms of his contemporaries affect Hawthorne as a writer? The answer is, probably, that they did not affect him at all. Hawthorne was invincibly modest; he often professed gratitude for favorable comments and sometimes declared that he hoped to profit by censures. He was always promising (to himself or to his friends) that he would attempt to meet the current demand and write something more " genial." In his later years he elected Whipple as his literary mentor, and appealed to him upon various problems with touching eagerness, quite as if he were not one of the most eminent authors of the day and presumably in a position to give, rather than to ask, advice. But his talent had, from its beginning, taken an unmistakable bent; and it pursued its own path with very little exterior influence and even with very little coercion from its possessor. Hawthorne apparently resigned himself to his fate. If he sometimes wished that he could write otherwise than he did he was quite convinced that it was impossible. Undoubtedly he owed something to the response of his public as well as to the kindness of his friends. If he had had no readers he would very possibly have written less. If Fields had not encouraged him he might not have attempted to write a novel. But the character of his work and its subject matter seems to have been equally unaffected by praise or by blame.

However, if Hawthorne was not affected by specific criticisms, he was indebted in a more general way to the support and sympathy of his day; and this in spite of the fact that most of his admirers deprecated his one indubitable masterpiece and chose as their favorite and as the best expression of his genius the novel which has least survived the test of the years. He belonged very much to his time and especially to his time in New England; and he was not only moulded by its larger influences but he received the benefit of its appreciation in a special fashion. In spite of the various words of disapproval which we have recorded, his contemporaries—his cultivated contemporaries—gave his work the ample suffrage which was dictated by its harmony with their tastes. In the matter of his style, for instance. All Hawthorne's critics praise it, and quite justly, for it is truly beautiful; but one sees that in the middle of the nineteenth century it made a more immediate appeal than it does now. Hawthorne's contemporaries had been brought up upon the productions of the Augustan age, they knew their *Spectator* and they were intimately aware of the "classic" touch—a touch which was then departing out of literature and which, in spite of some flattering English opinions, was not much more frequently found in America than in England. The purity and precision of Hawthorne's style were appreciated at once, even by those who would not have recognized beauty in the more loosely woven texture of Thackeray's "modern" style, because it was rendered agreeable by its association with the classical prose of English literature. Its much admired personal qualities were endeared by the same association. A vivid appreciation, in the case of the majority of his readers, rewarded his allegorizing, which later opinion, agreeing with Poe, has generally regarded as the bane of his genius. There were a few protests against his excessive employment of allegory but in general it was considered not only interesting but instructive. We might go on at length to name other traits in Hawthorne's writing—the " airiness " of his fancy and its extraordinary fecundity, for example—which were relatively more appreciated by the persons among whom he lived than by unprejudiced readers of later times; but we should merely be repeating what may be gathered from the opinions which we have quoted in the course of this study. The principal theme and motive of Hawthorne's work—its predominant interest in the spiritual—is of course very much of his age and for his age. There is probably no period in the whole history of the world when " spiritualities " (all kinds of spiritualities) possessed such general interest—especially in New England, of course, but appreciably in the rest of this country and in England. For the New England intellectual movement was no isolated phenomenon, though its concentration, its brilliance and its delightful local peculiarities have drawn attention to it. Similar tastes and similar thoughts existed elsewhere, and wherever they existed Hawthorne found especial admirers.

CHRONOLOGICAL LIST OF REVIEWS, NOTICES AND ARTICLES RELATING TO HAWTHORNE'S WORK 1828-1864

Ladies' Magazine (1: 526–527) November 1828. [Review of] Fanshawe. [Mrs. Sarah Josepha Hale].

Critic (1: 53–55) November 22, 1828. [Review of] Fanshawe. [William Leggett].

American Monthly Review (1: 154) February 1832. [Review of] The Token for 1832.

New England Magazine (9: 294–298) October 1835. [Review of] The Token and Atlantic Souvenir for 1836. [Park Benjamin].

Athenaeum (pp. 830–831) November 7, 1835. [Review of] The Token and Atlantic Souvenir for 1836. [Henry Fothergill Chorley].

American Monthly Magazine (n. s. 2: 406) October 1836. [Review of] The Token and Atlantic Souvenir for 1837. [Park Benjamin].

Salem Gazette (51: 2) March 14, 1837. [Review of] Twice-Told Tales.

North American Review (45: 59–73) July 1837. [Review of] Twice-Told Tales. [Henry Wadsworth Longfellow]. Reprinted in the Riverside Edition of Longfellow's works (1: 360–367).

Knickerbocker Magazine (10: 447–449) November 1837. [Review of] The Token and Atlantic Souvenir for 1838. [Lewis Gaylord Clark].

Family Magazine, or Monthly Abstract of General Knowledge (5: 280) November 1837. [Notice of] Twice-Told Tales.

American Monthly Magazine (n. s. 5: 281–283) March 1838. [Review of] Twice-Told Tales. [Charles Fenno Hoffman].

Democratic Review (3: 68–69) September 1838. Editor's Preface [to Hawthorne's Biographical Sketch of Jonathan Cilley]. [John O'Sullivan].

Christian Examiner (25: 182–190) November 1838. [Review of] Twice-Told Tales. A[ndrew] P[reston] P[eabody].

New York Review (4: 493) April 1839. [Notice of] The Gentle Boy.

Literary Gazette and Journal of Belles-Lettres (p. 302) June 22, 1839. [Notice of] The Gentle Boy.

Arcturus (1: 125–126) January 1841. [Review of] Grandfather's Chair. [Evert Augustus Duyckinck].

Arcturus (1: 330–337) May 1841. Nathaniel Hawthorne. E[vert] A[ugustus] D[uyckinck].

Arcturus (3: 152–155) January 1842. A Preamble to Nathaniel Hawthorne. [Evert Augustus Duyckinck].

Boston Miscellany of Literature and Fashion (1: 92) February 1842. [Review of] Twice-Told Tales 1842.

Knickerbocker (19: 282) March 1842. [Notice of] Twice-Told Tales. [Lewis Gaylord Clark].

Arcturus (3: 394) April 1842. [Review of] Twice-Told Tales. [Evert Augustus Duyckinck].

Boston Quarterly Review (5: 251–252) April 1842. [Review of] Twice-Told Tales. [Orestes Augustus Brownson].

Graham's Magazine (20: 254) April 1842. [Review of] Twice-Told Tales. [Edgar Allan Poe]. Reprinted in the Virginia Edition of Poe's works (11: 102–104).

North American Review (54: 496–499) April 1842. [Review of] Twice-Told Tales. [Henry Wadsworth Longfellow].

Graham's Magazine (20: 298–300) May 1842. [Another review of] Twice-Told Tales. [Edgar Allan Poe]. Virginia Edition (11: 104–113).

Pioneer (1: 41–42) January 1843. Hawthorne's Historical Tales for Youth. [James Russell Lowell].

Foreign and Colonial Quarterly Review (2: 458–488) October 1843. American Works of Fiction. [George James]. Reprinted in Littel's Living Age (2: 643–655) October 19, 1844.

Democratic Review (15: 585–586) December 1844. Marginalia. Edgar A[llan] Poe. Virginia Edition (16: 42–43).

Democratic Review (16: 376–384) April 1845. Nathaniel Hawthorne. [Evert Augustus Duyckinck].

Democratic Review (17: 212–219) September 1845. American Humor. [Evert Augustus Duyckinck].

Godey's Lady's Book (32: 194–195) May 1846. The Literati of New York City. Author's Introduction. Edgar A[llan] Poe. Virginia Edition (15: 3–4).

Athenaeum (pp. 807–808) August 8, 1846. [Review of] Mosses from an Old Manse. [Henry Fothergill Chorley].

American Review, a Whig Journal (4: 296–313) September 1846. Hawthorne. By Charles Winterfield. [Charles Wilkins Webber].

New Englander (5: 56–69) January 1847. Nathaniel Hawthorne. S[amuel] W[illiam] S[outhmayd] D[utton].

Blackwood's Magazine (62: 587–592) November 1847. The American Library.

Godey's Lady's Book (35: 252–256) November 1847. Tale-Writing—Nathaniel Hawthorne. [Review of] Twice-Told Tales and Mosses from an Old Manse. Edgar A[llan] Poe. Virginia Edition (13: 141–155).

Griswold, Rufus Wilmot. The Prose Writers of America. Philadelphia 1847. Nathaniel Hawthorne. (Pp. 470–482).

[Lowell, James Russell]. A Fable for Critics. . . . Boston 1848. [Verses on Hawthorne pp. 45–46]. In the Riverside Edition of Lowell's works (3: 32–33).

Literary World (6: 323–325) March 30, 1850. [Review of] The Scarlet Letter. [Evert Augustus Duyckinck].

New York Tribune, Supplement to the Daily Tribune (9: 2) April 1, 1850. [Review of] The Scarlet Letter. [George Ripley]. Reprinted in Littel's Living Age (25: 203–207) May 4, 1850.

Graham's Magazine (36: 345–346) May 1850. [Review of] The Scarlet Letter. [Edwin Percy Whipple].

Athenaeum (p. 634) June 15, 1850. [Review of] The Scarlet Letter. [Henry Fothergill Chorley].

North American Review (71: 135–148) July 1850. Hawthorne's Scarlet Letter. [Miss Anne W. Abbott].

Literary World (7: 125–127, 145–147) August 17 and 24, 1850. Hawthorne and his Mosses. By a Virginian Spending the Summer in Vermont. [Herman Melville].

Massachusetts Quarterly Review (3: 484–500) September 1850. [Review of] The Scarlet Letter. [George Bailey Loring].

Brownson's Quarterly Review (7: 528–532) October 1850. The Scarlet Letter. [Orestes Augustus Brownson].

Harper's New Monthly Magazine (2: 140) December 1850. [Notice of] Grandfather's Chair.

Literary World (7: 455) December 7, 1850. [Notice of] True Stories from History and Biography. [Evert Augustus Duyckinck].

Church Review (3: 489–511) January 1851. The Writings of Hawthorne. A[rthur] C[leveland] Coxe. Partially reprinted: Mordell, Albert. Notorious Literary Attacks. New York 1926. (Pp. 122–137).

Graham's Magazine (38: 134) February 1851. [Notice of] True Stories from History and Biography.

Knickerbocker (37: 264–265) March 1851. [Notice of] Twice-Told Tales, new edition. [Lewis Gaylord Clark].

Literary World (8: 249–250) March 29, 1851. The Founder of the " House of the Seven Gables." A Passage from Hawthorne's Forthcoming Romance.

Graham's Magazine (38: 342–343) April 1851. [Review of] The Memorial.

Harper's Magazine (2: 712) April 1851. [Notice of] Twice-Told Tales.

Southern Quarterly Review (n. s. 3: 571–572) April 1851. [Notice of] True Stories from History and Biography.

Literary World (8: 334–335) April 26, 1851. The House of the Seven Gables. [Evert Augustus Duyckinck].

Harper's Magazine (2: 855–856) May 1851. [Notice of] The House of the Seven Gables.

International Monthly Magazine (3: 156–160) May 1851. Nathaniel Hawthorne. [Rufus Wilmot Griswold].

Knickerbocker (37: 455–457) May 1851. [Notice of] The House of the Seven Gables. [Lewis Gaylord Clark].

Athenaeum (pp. 545–547) May 24, 1851. [Review of] The House of the Seven Gables. [Henry Fothergill Chorley].

Graham's Magazine (38: 467–468, 469) June 1851. [Review of] The House of the Seven Gables and Twice-Told Tales. [Edwin Percy Whipple].

Southern Literary Messenger (17: 344–349) June 1851. Nathaniel Hawthorne. Henry T[heodore] Tuckerman. Reprinted: Tuckerman, Henry T. Mental Portraits. London 1853. (Pp. 250–270). Littel's Living Age (81: 518–524) June 11, 1864.

Southern Quarterly Review (n. s. 4: 265–266) July 1851. [Notice of] The House of the Seven Gables.

Universalist Quarterly (8: 273–293) July 1851. The Works of Hawthorne. A[mory] D[wight] M[ayo].

Literary World (9: 424–425) November 29, 1851. Hawthorne's Wonder-Book for Girls and Boys. [Evert Augustus Duyckinck].

Southern Quarterly Review (n. s. 5: 262) January 1852. [Notice of] The Snow Image.

Today: A Boston Literary Journal (1: 8) January 1852. [Notice of] The Snow Image.

Literary World (10: 22–27) January 10, 1852. New Tales by Hawthorne. [Evert Augustus Duyckinck].

New Monthly Magazine (94: 202–207) February 1852. Nathaniel Hawthorne. By Sir Nathaniel. Reprinted in Littel's Living Age (33: 17–19) April 3, 1852.

Graham's Magazine (40: 443) April 1852. [Review of] The Snow Image. [Edwin Percy Whipple].

Revue des Deux Mondes (14: 337–365) April 15, 1852. Poetes et Romanciers Americains. Nathaniel Hawthorne. Paul Emile Durand Forgues.

Today (1: 296, 344) May 8, May 29, 1852. Literary Notes. [Notes on The Blithedale Romance].

Literary World (10: 391–392) June 5, 1852. Hawthorne.

Eliza Cook's Journal (7: 121–124) June 19, 1852. Nathaniel Hawthorne.

New Monthly Magazine (95: 334–343) July 1852. [Review of] The Blithedale Romance. Reprinted in Littel's Living Age (34: 327–332) August 14, 1852.

Spectator (25: 637–638) July 3, 1852. [Review of] The Blithedale Romance. Reprinted partially in Littel's Living Age (34: 332) August 14, 1852.

Athenaeum (pp. 741–743) July 10, 1852. [Review of] The Blithedale Romance. [Henry Fothergill Chorley].

Today (2: 24) July 10, 1852. Literary Notes. [Note on the Life of Pierce].

Today (2: 42) July 17, 1852. [Review of] The Blithedale Romance.

Literary World (11: 52–54) July 24, 1852. Hawthorne's Blithedale Romance.

Democratic Review (31: 276–288) September 1852. Hawthorne's Life of Pierce. Perspective.

Graham's Magazine (41: 333–334) September 1852. [Review of] The Blithedale Romance. [Edwin Percy Whipple].

Today (2: 177–181) September 18, 1852. Nathaniel Hawthorne. [Charles Hale].

Literary World (11: 195–196) September 25, 1852. Hawthorne's Life of Franklin Pierce. [Evert Augustus Duyckinck].

Brownson's Quarterly Review (n. s. 6: 561–564) October 1852. [Review of] The Blithedale Romance. [Orestes Augustus Brownson].

New Quarterly Review (1: 413–415) October 1852. [Review of] The Blithedale Romance.

Southern Quarterly Review (n. s. 6: 543) October 1852. [Notice of] The Blithedale Romance.

Westminster Review (58: 592–598; American Edition 35: 218–312) October 1852. Contemporary Literature of America. Fiction.

Today (2: 232) October 9, 1852. Literary Notes. [Note on the Life of Pierce].

American Whig Review (16: 417–424) November 1852. The Blithedale Romance.

Literary World (11: 341) November 27, 1852. Homes of American Authors. Second Notice. [Evert Augustus Duyckinck].

Revue des Deux Mondes (4: 809–841) December 1, 1852. Un Roman Socialiste en Amerique. Emile Montegut.

Today (2: 407) December 25, 1852. Literary Notes. [Note on The Blithedale Romance].

Mitford, Mary Russell. Recollections of a Literary Life. New York 1852. American Prose Writers. Nathaniel Hawthorne. (Pp. 515–531).

National Magazine (2: 17–24) January 1853. Nathaniel Hawthorne. [Richard Henry Stoddard].

North American Review (76: 227–248) January 1852. Nathaniel Hawthorne. [Review of] The Blithedale Romance and The House of the Seven Gables. [Andrew Preston Peabody].

Harper's Magazine (6: 846–850) May 1853. Editor's Easy Chair. [Hawthorne as Consul]. [Donald Grant Mitchell].

New Monthly Magazine (98: 202–212) June 1853. American Authorship. By Sir Nathaniel. No. III. Nathaniel Hawthorne. Reprinted in Littel's Living Age (38: 154–160) July 16, 1853; and in Eclectic Magazine (29: 481–488) August 1853.

Graham's Magazine (43: 333–334) September 1853. [Review of] Inglewood Tales [*sic*].

Literary World (13: 99–101) September 10, 1853. Hawthorne's Tanglewood Tales. [Edwin Percy Whipple].

North British Review (20: 81–99) November 1853. American Novels. Reprinted in Littel's Living Age (40: 51–59) January 7, 1854.

Curtis, George William. Homes of American Authors. New York 1853. Nathaniel Hawthorne. (Pp. 289–313).

Tuckerman, Henry T. A Sketch of American Literature. In Outlines of English Literature by Thomas B. Shaw, Philadelphia 1853. (Pp. 456–457).

Whipple, Edwin Percy. Lectures on Subjects Connected with Literature and Life. Boston 1853. The Ludicrous Side of Life. (Pp. 122–155).

Yale Literary Magazine (19: 252–255) June 1854. Nathaniel Hawthorne.

Bungay, George Washington. Off-Hand Takings; or Crayon Studies of the Noticeable Men of Our Age. New York 1854. Nathaniel Hawthorne. (Pp. 210–213).

Giles, Henry. Illustrations of Genius. Boston 1854. The Scarlet Letter. (Pp. 66–90).

Tait's Edinburgh Magazine (22: 33–41) January 1855. Reading Raids. I. American Literature: Poe; Hawthorne.

Blackwood's Magazine (77: 562–566) May 1855. Modern Novelists Great and Small. Reprinted in Littel's Living Age (45: 649–652) June 16, 1855.

Harvard Magazine (1: 330–335) July 1855. Hawthorne. [Charles Francis Adams].

Dublin University Magazine (46: 463–469) October 1855. Nathaniel Hawthorne. Reprinted in Eclectic Magazine (36: 996–1001) November 1855.

Duyckinck, Evert A. and Duyckinck, George L. Cyclopaedia of American Literature from the Earliest Period to the Present Day. New York 1855. Nathaniel Hawthorne (2: 503–507).

Tait's Edinburgh Magazine (27: 756–757) December 1856. Nathaniel Hawthorne.

Gilman, Samuel. Contributions to Literature. Boston 1856. A Day of Disappointment in Salem. By an Admirer of " Twice-Told Tales." (Pp. 474–496).

Revue Contemporaine (31: 633–663) May 30, 1857. Les Conteurs Americains. Nathaniel Hawthorne. Lucien Etienne.

Allibone, S. Austen. A Critical Dictionary of English Literature, and British and American Authors, Living and Deceased, from the Earliest Accounts to the Middle of the Nineteenth Century. 2 v. Philadelphia 1859. Nathaniel Hawthorne (1: 804–806).

Hood, Edwin Paxton (ed). Master Minds of the West: Their Best Poems, Thoughts, Essays and Tales. London (1859). Nathaniel Hawthorne. (Pp. 505–558).

Athenaeum (pp. 296–297) March 3, 1860. [Review of] Transformation. [Henry Fothergill Chorley].

Saturday Review (9: 341–342) March 17, 1860. [Review of] Transformation. Reprinted in Littel's Living Age (65: 323–325) May 12, 1860.

Examiner (p. 197) March 31, 1860. [Review of] Transformation. [Henry Bright].

Atlantic Monthly (5: 509–510) April 1860. [Review of] The Marble Faun. [James Russell Lowell].

North American Review (90: 557–558) April 1860. [Review of] The Marble Faun. [Charles Card Smith].

Westminster Review (73: 624–627; American Edition 50: 338–347) April 1860. Contemporary Literature. Belles Lettres. [Review of Transformation].

Art-Journal (p. 127) April 1, 1860. [Review of] Transformation. [Samuel Carter Hall].

The Times (p. 5) April 7, 1860. [Review of] Transformation.

Atlantic Monthly (5: 614–622) May 1860. Nathaniel Hawthorne. [Edwin Percy Whipple]. Reprinted in: Whipple, Edwin Percy. Character and Characteristic Men. Boston 1886. (Pp. 218–242).

Harper's Magazine (20: 845–846) May 1860. Editor's Easy Chair. [A Bust of Hawthorne].

New Englander (18: 441–452) May 1860. The Marble Faun. [Miss Eliza W. Robbins].

Dublin University Magazine (55: 679–688) June 1860. American Imaginings. [Review of Transformation].

Universal Review (3: 742–771) June 1860. Nathaniel Hawthorne. Reprinted in Littel's Living Age (65: 707–723) June 23, 1860.

North British Review (33: 165–185) August 1860. Imaginative Literature. The Author of Adam Bede and Nathaniel Hawthorne.

Revue des Deux Mondes (28: 668–703) August 1, 1860. Un Romancier Pessimiste en Amerique. Nathaniel Hawthorne. Emile Montegut.

The Crayon (7: 299–301) October 1860. Sketchings. Hawthorne in Relation to Art.

National Review (11: 453–481) October 1860. Nathaniel Hawthorne. [Richard Holt Hutton]. Partially reprinted in Littel's Living Age (68: 217–232) January 26, 1861.

Smiles, Samuel. Brief Biographies. London 1860. Nathaniel Hawthorne. (Pp. 256–269).

New Englander (19: 860–870) October 1861. The Marble Faun; An Allegory, with a Key to its Interpretation. [Mrs. Martha Tyler Gale]. Reprinted in the New Englander (56: 26–36) January 1892.

Probiblion (1: 21) December 1861. Hawthorne and Evangeline. W. A. J. Also in Notes and Queries (3d ser. 1: 287) April 12, 1862.

Yale Literary Magazine (28: 300–303) June 1863. Nathaniel Hawthorne.

Reader (2: 336–338) September 26, 1863. Nathaniel Hawthorne on England and the English. Reprinted in Littel's Living Age (79: 243–250) November 7, 1863.

North American Review (97: 588–589) October 1863. [Review of] Our Old Home.

Reader (2: 367–368) October 3, 1863. American Views of the English Character.

Examiner, October 17, 1863. [Review of] Our Old Home. [Henry Bright].

Punch (45: 161) October 17, 1863. A Handful of Hawthorn. Reprinted in Littel's Living Age (79: 339–340).

Blackwood's Magazine (94: 610–623) November 1863. Hawthorne on England. Partially reprinted in Littel's Living Age (80: 15–16) January 2, 1864.

Continental Monthly (4: 595) November 1863. [Review of] Our Old Home.

The Times (p. 10) November 9, 1863. [Review of] Our Old Home.

Botta, Anne C. Lynch. Handbook of Universal Literature. Boston 1863. (Hawthorne, p. 537).

Bentley's Miscellany. London 1863. Imperfect Criminals. A Vexed Question. Francis Jacox. Reprinted in Littel's Living Age (80: 23–27) January 2, 1864.

Christian Remembrancer (47: 165–188) January 1864. Mr. Hawthorne on England and the English. Reprinted in Littel's Living Age (81: 99–114).

Quarterly Review (115: 42–68) January 1864. New Englanders and the Old Home. Reprinted in Littel's Living Age (80: 339–353) February 20, 1864.

Examiner (pp. 387–388) June 18, 1864. Nathaniel Hawthorne's Death. [Henry Bright]. Reprinted in Littel's Living Age (82: 222) July 30, 1864.

Atlantic Monthly (14: 98–101) July 1864. Hawthorne. [Introducing a scene from The Dolliver Romance]. [Oliver Wendell Holmes].

Macmillan's Magazine (10: 241–246) July 1864. Nathaniel Hawthorne. Edward Dicey.

Spectator (37: 705–706) July 18, 1864. Nathaniel Hawthorne. [Richard Holt Hutton]. Reprinted in Littel's Living Age (82: 219–222) July 30, 1864; and in three collections of essays by R. H. Hutton: Essays, Theological and Literary. 2 v. London 1871; Essays in Literary Criticism. Philadelphia 1876; Literary Essays. London 1888.

Atlantic Monthly (14: 169–170) August 1864. Concord. [Poem on Hawthorne's funeral]. Henry W. Longfellow. In the Riverside Edition of Longfellow's works (3: 130–132). Hawthorne.

Fraser's Magazine (70: 245–264) August 1864. The Transcendentalists of Concord. [Moncure Daniel Conway]. Reprinted in Littel's Living Age (83: 99–105) October 15, 1864.

Harper's Magazine (29: 405) August 1864. Editor's Easy Chair. (Hawthorne's death). [George William Curtis].

Spectator (pp. 1075–1076) September 17, 1864. Mr. Hawthorne's Last Fragment. [Richard Holt Hutton]. Reprinted in Littel's Living Age (83: 147–149) October 22, 1864.

North American Review (99: 539–557) October 1864. The Works of Nathaniel Hawthorne. [George William Curtis].

Smith, Alexander. Dreamthorp. London 1864. A Shelf in My Bookcase. (Pp. 191–213).

GENERAL BIBLIOGRAPHY

Alcott, Amos Bronson. Concord Days. Boston 1872.

Allibone, S. Austin. A Critical Dictionary of English Literature and British and American Authors Living and Deceased, from the Earliest Accounts to the Middle of the Nineteenth Century. 3 v. Philadelphia 1859. With Supplement by John Foster Kirk. 2 v. Philadelphia 1891.

Appleton's Cyclopaedia of American Biography. 12 v. New York 1887–1931.

The Atlantic Souvenir, a Christmas and New Year's Offering. Philadelphia 1826–1832.

Beers, Henry A. Nathaniel Parker Willis. Boston 1885. (American Men of Letters.)

Belden, H. M. Poe's Critique of Hawthorne. Anglia (23: 376–404) 1910.

Bridge, Horatio. Personal Recollections of Nathaniel Hawthorne. New York 1893.

Brooks, Van Wyck. The Flowering of New England. New York 1936.

Browne, Nina E. Bibliography of Nathaniel Hawthorne. Boston 1905.

Brownell, W. C. American Prose Masters. New York 1909.

Brownson, H. F. Orestes A. Brownson's Life. 3 v. Detroit 1898–1900.

Brownson, Orestes Augustus. Works: Collected and Arranged by H. F. Brownson. 20 v. Detroit 1882–1887.

The Cambridge History of American Literature. Edited by N. P. Trent and others. 4 v. New York 1917–1921.

Cary, Edward. George William Curtis. Boston 1894. (American Men of Letters.)

Charvat, William. The Origins of American Critical Thought 1810–1835. Philadelphia 1936.

Chorley, Henry Fothergill. Autobiography, Memoirs and Letters of Henry Fothergill Chorley. Edited by H. E. Hewlett. London 1873.

Conway, M. D. Hawthorne. His Uncollected Tales in the Token Beginning with 1830. New York Times Literary Supplement (pp. 397–398) June 8, 1901.

Conway, Moncure Daniel. Life of Nathaniel Hawthorne. New York 1890. (Great Writers.)

[Cooper, James Fenimore]. Home as Found. 2 v. Philadelphia 1838.

[Cooper, James Fenimore]. Notions of the Americans Picked up by a Travelling Bachelor. 2 v. Philadelphia 1828.

Curtis, George William. Ars Recte Vivendi; Being Essays Contributed to The Easy Chair. New York 1898.

Curtis, George William. From The Easy Chair. New York 1892.

Derby, J. C. Fifty Years Among Authors, Books and Publishers. New York 1884.

The Dictionary of American Biography. 20 v. New York 1928–1936.

The Dictionary of National Biography. London (n. e. 1921–1927).

Eckerman, D. C. A Bibliography of Nathaniel Hawthorne. New Haven 1930. (Unpublished.)

Emerson, Ralph Waldo. Complete Works. . . . 11 v. Boston 1889–1891. (Riverside Edition.)

Emerson, Ralph Waldo. Journals . . . with Annotations. Edited by E. W. Emerson and W. E. Forbes. 10 v. Boston 1909–1914.

Faxon, Frederick Winthrop. Literary Annuals and Gift-Books. A Bibliography with Descriptive Introduction. Boston 1912.

Fields, Mrs. Annie. Nathaniel Hawthorne. Boston 1899. (Beacon Biographies.)

Fields, J. T. Biographical Notes and Personal Sketches. Boston 1881.

Fields, James Thomas. Hawthorne. Boston 1876.

Fields, James Thomas. Yesterdays with Authors. Boston 1872.

Frothingham, Octavius Brooks. George Ripley. Boston 1882. (American Men of Letters.)

Godwin, Parke. A Biography of William Cullen Bryant. 2 v. New York 1883.

Goodrich, S. G. Recollections of a Lifetime; or, Men and Things I Have Seen. New York 1856.

Hall, S. C. Retrospect of a Long Life, from 1815 to 1883. . . . New York 1883.

Hawthorne, Julian. A Group of Hawthorne Letters. Harper's Magazine (108: 602-607) March 1904.

Hawthorne, Julian. Hawthorne and his Circle. New York 1903.

Hawthorne, Julian. Nathaniel Hawthorne and his Wife. A Biography. 2 v. Boston 1885.

Hawthorne, Nathaniel. The American Notebooks by Nathaniel Hawthorne, Based upon the Original Manuscripts in the Pierpont Morgan Library and Edited by Randall Stewart. New Haven 1932.

Hawthorne, Nathaniel. Complete Works. . . . Edited by George Parsons Lathrop. 13 v. Boston 1883–1889. (Riverside Edition.)

Hawthorne, Nathaniel. Hawthorne in the Boston Custom House. Extracts from his Private Letters. Atlantic Monthly (21: 106–111) February 1868.

Hawthorne, Nathaniel. Love Letters of Nathaniel Hawthorne 1839–1841, 1841–1863. 2 v. Chicago 1907. (Privately printed.)

Hawthorne, Nathaniel. Unpublished Letters of Nathaniel Hawthorne. Athenaeum (pp. 191, 192, 225) August 10 and 17, 1889.

Hawthorne, Nathaniel. Works. . . . With an Analytical Index and Sketch of Hawthorne's Life by Evangeline Maria O'Connor. 25 v. Boston 1875–1883. (Little Classic Edition.)

Hawthorne, Nathaniel. Writings. . . . With an Introduction by Rose Hawthorne Lathrop and Bibliography by H. E. Scudder. 22 v. Boston 1900. (Autograph Edition.)

Hawthorne, Mrs. Sophia. Notes in England and Italy. New York 1869.

Holmes, Oliver Wendell. Works. . . . 14 v. Boston 1891–1892. (Riverside Edition.)

Howells, William Dean. Life in Letters of William Dean Howells. Edited by Mildred Howells. 2 v. New York 1928.

Howells, W. D. Literary Friends and Acquaintance. A Personal Retrospect of American Authorship. New York 1900.

Howells, W. D. My Literary Passions. New York 1895.

Hutton, Richard Holt. Essays, Theological and Literary. 2 v. London 1871.

James, Henry, Jr. Hawthorne. New York 1879.

James, Henry. Partial Portraits. London 1888.

Jepson, George Edward. Hawthorne in the Boston Custom House. Bookman (19: 573) August 1904.

Joline, Adrian H. Meditations of an Autograph Collector. New York 1902.

Jones, H. M. American Comment on George Sand 1837–1848. American Literature (3: 389–407) January 1932.

Lathrop, George Parsons. Study of Hawthorne. Boston 1876.

Lathrop, Mrs. Rose. Memories of Hawthorne. Boston 1897.

Longfellow, Henry Wadsworth. Complete Works . . . with Bibliographical and Critical Notes. 11 v. Boston 1893–1903. (Riverside Edition.)

Longfellow, Henry Wadsworth. Life of Henry Wadsworth Longfellow, with Extracts from his Journals and Correspondence. Edited by Samuel Longfellow. 2 v. Boston 1886.

Lounsbury, Thomas R. James Fenimore Cooper. Boston 1883. (American Men of Letters.)

Lowell, James Russell. Early Prose Writings . . . with a Prefatory Note by Dr. Hale of Boston and an Introduction by Walter Littlefield. London 1903.

Lowell, James Russell. Letters. . . . Edited by C. E. Norton. 2 v. New York 1894.

Lowell, James Russell. New Letters of James Russell Lowell. Edited by M. A. De Wolfe Howe. New York 1932.

Lowell, James Russell. Works. . . . 11 v. Boston 1890–1892. (Riverside Edition.)

Melville, Herman. Some Personal Letters of Herman Melville. Edited by Meade Minnigerode. New Haven 1922.

Motley, John Lathrop. The Correspondence of John Lathrop Motley. Edited by G. W. Curtis. 2 v. New York 1889.

Mott, Frank Luther. American Magazines 1865–1880. Iowa City 1928.

Mott, Frank Luther. A History of American Magazines 1741–1850. New York 1930.

Parrington, Vernon Louis. Main Currents in American Thought; An Interpretation of American Literature from the Beginnings to 1920. 2 v. New York 1927.

Pattee, Fred Lewis. The First Century of American Literature 1770–1870. New York 1935.

Perry, Bliss. Park-Street Papers. Boston 1908.

Poe, Edgar Allan. Complete Works. . . . Edited by J. A. Harrison. 17 v. New York 1902–1903. (Virginia Edition.)

Poole, William Frederick. An Index to Periodical Literature. Boston 1882.

Quinn, Arthur Hobson. American Fiction; An Historical and Critical Survey. New York 1936.

Scudder, H. E. James Russell Lowell. A Biography. 2 v. Boston 1901.

Stewart, Randall. Hawthorne and Politics: Unpublished Letters of William B. Pike. New England Quarterly (5: 237–263) April 1932.

Stoddard, Richard Henry. Recollections Personal and Literary. Edited by Ripley Hitchcock. New York 1903.

Sumner, Charles. Memoir and Letters of Charles Sumner. Edited by Edward L. Pierce. Boston 1877.

Thompson, Ralph. American Literary Annuals and Gift-Books 1825–1865. New York 1936.

Thoreau, Henry David. Familiar Letters of Henry David Thoreau. Edited by F. B. Sanborn. Boston 1895.

Ticknor, Caroline. Hawthorne and his Publisher. Boston 1913.

Ticknor, George. Life, Letters and Journals of George Ticknor. Boston 1877.

The Token, a Christmas and New Year's Present. Edited by S. G. Goodrich. (By N. P. Willis in 1829.) 1828–1832. The Token and Atlantic Souvenir, a Christmas and New Year's Present. Edited by S. G. Goodrich. Boston 1833–1841.

Tuckerman, Henry T. Essays, Biographical and Critical; or Studies of Character. Boston 1857.

(Tuckerman, Henry Theodore). Leaves from the Diary of a Dreamer: Found among his Papers. London 1853.

Wendell, Barrett. Literary History of America. New York 1900.

Whipple, Edwin Percy. Character and Characteristic Men. Boston 1886.

Whipple, Edwin Percy. Essays and Reviews. 2 v. Boston 1848.

Whipple, Edwin Percy. Recollections of Eminent Men with Other Papers, with an Introduction by C. A. Bartol. Boston 1887.

Williams, Stanley T. American Literature. Philadelphia 1933.

Willis, N. P. Prose Works. . . . Philadelphia 1854.

Woodberry, George E. Nathaniel Hawthorne. Boston 1902. (American Men of Letters.)

Woodberry, George E. The Life of Edgar Allan Poe, Personal and Literary, with his Chief Correspondence with Men of Letters. 2 v. Boston 1909.